Designing Learning

New lecturers, part-time teachers and graduate teaching assistants are often required to both deliver an existing course and design their own teaching based on a module description. But where do they start?

Underpinned by sound theory, *Designing Learning* is a practical guide that aims to help busy professionals design, develop and deliver a course, from module outline to effective teaching. Illustrated with useful checklists and action points, this book covers the essentials of designing learning:

- supporting and promoting student learning
- matching content to outcomes
- selecting effective teaching and learning methods
- assessment that supports and promotes learning and provides feedback
- learning materials and resources for diverse learners
- C&IT tools and how to use them best
- creating an inclusive learning environment
- managing and evaluating your course
- quality enhancement and assurance processes.

Guided by principles of good practice and reflecting the educational research that underpins them, this book is essential reading for anyone new to teaching in higher education.

Christopher Butcher is Principal Academic Staff Development Officer, in the Staff and Departmental Development Unit at the University of Leeds. National Teaching Fellow (2005).

Clara Davies is Senior Academic Staff Development Officer at the University of Leeds.

Melissa Highton is Senior Staff Development Officer responsible for staff development in the use of C&IT in learning, teaching and assessment at the University of Leeds.

Key Guides for Effective Teaching in Higher Education Series
Edited by Kate Exley

This indispensable series is aimed at new lecturers, postgraduate students who have teaching time, graduate teaching assistants, part-time tutors and demonstrators, as well as experienced teaching staff who may feel it is time to review their skills in teaching and learning.

Titles in this series will provide the teacher in higher education with practical, realistic guidance on the various different aspects of their teaching role, which is underpinned not only by current research in the field, but also by the extensive experience of individual authors, with a keen eye kept on the limitations and opportunities therein. By bridging a gap between academic theory and practice, all titles will provide generic guidance on teaching, learning and assessment issues which is then brought to life through the use of short illustrative examples drawn from a range of disciplines. All titles in this series will:

■ represent up-to-date thinking and incorporate the use of communication and information technologies (C&IT) where appropriate;
■ consider methods and approaches for teaching and learning when there is an increasing diversity in learning and a growth in student numbers;
■ encourage reflective practice and self-evaluation, and a means of developing the skills of teaching, learning and assessment;
■ provide links and references to further work on the topic and research evidence where appropriate.

Titles in the series will prove invaluable whether they are used for self-study or as part of a formal induction programme on teaching in higher education, and will also be of relevance to teaching staff working in further education settings.

Other titles in this series:

Assessing Skills and Practice
  – Sally Brown and Ruth Pickford
Assessing Students' Written Work: Marking Essays and Reports
  – Catherine Haines
Developing Your Teaching: Ideas, Insight and Action
  – Peter Kahn and Lorraine Walsh
Giving a Lecture: From Presenting to Teaching
  – Kate Exley and Reg Dennick
Small Group Teaching
  – Kate Exley and Reg Dennick
Using C&IT to Support Teaching
  – Paul Chin

Designing Learning

From module outline
to effective teaching

Christopher Butcher, Clara Davies and Melissa Highton

Routledge
Taylor & Francis Group

LONDON AND NEW YORK

First published 2006 by Routledge
2 Park Square, Milton Park, Abingdon, Oxon OX14 4RN

Simultaneously published in the USA and Canada
by Routledge
270 Madison Avenue, New York, NY 10016

Routledge is an imprint of the Taylor & Francis Group, an informa business

© 2006 Christopher Butcher, Clara Davies and Melissa Highton

Typeset in Perpetua and Bell Gothic by
Florence Production Ltd, Stoodleigh, Devon

British Library Cataloguing in Publication Data
A catalogue record for this book is available from the British Library

Library of Congress Cataloging in Publication Data
A catalog record for this book has been requested.

ISBN10: 0–415–38031–6 (hbk)
ISBN10: 0–415–38030–8 (pbk)
ISBN10: 0–203–96848–4 (ebk)

ISBN13: 978–0–415–38031–7 (hbk)
ISBN13: 978–0–415–38030–0 (pbk)
ISBN13: 978–0–203–96848–2 (ebk)

Contents

Illustrations

FIGURES

TABLES

Foreword

In this book we aim to help you with the demanding task of designing, teaching and managing student learning in higher education. As well as providing helpful tips, ideas and guidance, we offer a structure and rationale to underpin all aspects of designing learning, from module outline to effective teaching, to give balance between sound theory and practical advice.

While the book tells the whole story in a structured and ordered way, each chapter stands alone. This gives you the choice over how to access the information, and we have cross-referenced chapters in order to provide additional pathways through the text. At the end of each chapter, there is a range of further reading and resources, as appropriate.

We start by looking at the higher education context in its broadest sense in order to give a framework for the more detailed discussion that follows. The sense of a dynamic and challenging world is prevalent throughout the chapter as we look at influences, trends and drivers over the last few decades, as well as current imperatives and initiatives.

In Chapter 2 – How your teaching fits into the bigger picture – we start to focus down and offer several curriculum design models, and introduce a number of reference points that must be taken account of when planning courses. Two important threads that permeate the book should become clear from the chapter: the use of communication and information technology (C&IT) and the need for inclusivity in the design process. Figure 2.1 includes eight aspects: one (rationale) is discussed at the end of the chapter and the other seven provide the structure for the rest of the book. This approach illuminates the emphasis on coherence – constructive alignment – that pervades the book.

Chapter 3 asks 'What are your students supposed to learn and be able to do?' and gives guidance on writing aims and learning outcomes. The emphasis here is their use for guiding learning rather than fulfilling some bureaucratic quality assurance procedure. With this in mind, Chapter 4 – Matching your content to outcomes, and not the other way around – asks you to think about the difficult process of selecting content. We say 'difficult' because deciding what not to include is as important as selecting the disciplinary knowledge and insights that you will use.

The focus of Chapter 5 is Horses for courses – selecting the appropriate teaching and learning methods. While some of these might be dictated (by available facilities, resources and tradition), we ask you to consider how you can be most effective and efficient in the approaches you use. In addition, a comprehensive structure for session planning is provided.

Chapter 6 – Matching your assessment to outcomes – asks how we can find out whether students have learned anything. We look at the why?, what?, when? and how? of assessment. A vital aspect of this survey is the process of giving students feedback on their work in order to provide both an indication of the standard achieved and how they can improve next time.

Chapters 7 and 8 – Learning materials and resources for diverse learners and Supporting your learners – relate to the 'environment' aspect of the design cycle. Matching students' needs through the learning materials that you provide (handouts and web resources, for example), while staying within the copyright laws is the issue for Chapter 7. Chapter 8 reviews the range of support mechanisms that we need to employ and be aware of: academic and pastoral tutoring; progress files; skills development; and the range of agencies from accommodation to careers and medical to religious.

The penultimate chapter – Managing your course – considers best practice in the knotty issue of providing information and documentation to students in a timely and user-friendly way. The place of the Virtual Learning Environment (VLE) as a course management tool and using the Internet as a teaching/learning resource are key parts of this.

The final chapter – Does the course work? – considers approaches to the evaluation and review of courses. A why?, what?, when? and how? structure to the text ensures that all the issues are considered.

We hope you will find the book a useful guide and reference.

Series preface

This series of books grew out of discussions with new lecturers and part-time teachers in universities and colleges who were keen to develop their teaching skills. However, experienced colleagues may also enjoy and find merit in the books, particularly the discussions about current issues that are impacting on teaching and learning in further and higher education, e.g. widening participation, disability legislation and the integration of C&IT in teaching.

New lecturers are now likely to be required by their institutions to take part in teaching development programmes. This frequently involves attending workshops, investigating teaching through mini-projects and reflecting on their practice. Many teaching programmes ask participants to develop their own teaching portfolios and to provide evidence of their developing skills and understanding. Scholarship of teaching is usually an important aspect of the teaching portfolio. New teachers can be asked to consider their own approach to teaching in relation to the wider literature, research findings, and theory of teaching and learning. However, when people are beginning their teaching careers a much more pressing need may be to design and deliver an effective teaching session for tomorrow. Hence, the intention of this series is to provide a complementary mix of very practical teaching tips and guidance, together with a strong basis and clear rationale for their use.

In many institutions the numbers of part-time and occasional teachers actually outnumber the full-time staff. Yet the provision of formal training and development for part-time teachers is more sporadic and variable across the sector. As a result, this diverse group of educators can feel isolated and left out of the updating and support offered to their full-time counterparts. Never has there been so many part-time teachers involved in the design and delivery of courses, the support and guidance of students, and the monitoring and assessment of learning. The group includes the thousands of postgraduate students who work as laboratory demonstrators, problem-class tutors, project supervisors and class teachers. The group includes clinicians, lawyers and professionals who contribute their specialist knowledge and skills to enrich the learning experience for many vocational and professional course students. The group also includes the many hourly paid and jobbing tutors who have helped full-time staff to cope with the expansion and diversification of further and higher education.

Universities sometimes struggle to know how many part-time staff they employ to teach and, as a group, occasional teachers are notoriously difficult to contact systematically through university and college communication systems. Part-time and occasional teachers often have other roles and responsibilities, and teaching is a small but important part of what they do each day. Many part-time tutors would not expect to undertake the full range of teaching activities of full-time staff, but may well do lots of tutoring or lots of class teaching but never lecture or supervise (or vice versa). So the series provides short practical books that focus very squarely on different teaching roles and activities. The first four books published are:

- *Assessing Students' Written Work: Marking Essays and Reports*
- *Giving a Lecture: From Presenting to Teaching*
- *Small Group Teaching*
- *Using C&IT to Support Teaching*

The books are all very practical with detailed discussion of teaching techniques and methods, but they are based on educational theory and research findings. Articles are referenced, further readings and related web sites are given, and workers in the field are quoted and acknowledged. To this end, Dr George Brown has been commissioned to produce an associated web-based guide on Student Learning that can be freely accessed by readers to accompany the books and provide a substantial foundation for the teaching and assessment practices discussed and recommended for the texts.

There is much enthusiasm and support here too for the excellent work currently being carried out by the Higher Education Academy subject centres within discipline groupings (indeed, individual subject centres are suggested as sources of further information throughout these volumes). The need to provide part-time tutors with realistic connections with their own disciplines is keenly felt by all the authors in the series and 'how it might work in your department' examples are given at the end of many of the activity-based chapters. However, there is, no doubt, some merit in sharing teaching developments across the boundaries of disciplines, culture and country as many of the problems in the tertiary education sector are themselves widely shared.

UNDERLYING THEMES

The use of communication and information technology (C&IT) to enrich student learning and to help manage the workload of teachers is a recurring theme in the series. I acknowledge that not all teachers may have access to state-of-the-art teaching resources and facilities. However, the use of virtual learning environments, e-learning provision and audio-visual presentation media is now widespread in universities.

The books also acknowledge and try to help new teachers respond to the growing and changing nature of the student population. Students with non-traditional backgrounds, international students, students who have disabilities or special needs are encouraged through the government's widening participation agenda to take part in further and higher education. The books seek to advise teachers on current legislative requirements and offer guidance on recommended good practice on teaching diverse groups of students.

These were our goals, and I and my co-authors sincerely hope these volumes prove to be a helpful resource for colleagues, both new and experienced, in further and higher education.

Abbreviations

BDA	British Dyslexia Association
BUFVC	British Universities Film and Video Council
C&IT	communication and information technology
CEQ	Course Evaluation Questionnaire
CETL	Centre for the Enhancement of Teaching and Learning
CLA	Copyright Licensing Agency
DDA	Disability Discrimination Act
DED	Disability Equality Duty
FHEQ	Framework for Higher Education Qualifications
HE	higher education
HEI	higher education institution
HESA	Higher Education Statistics Agency
HEFCE	Higher Education Funding Council of England
IT	information technology
JISC	Joint Information Systems Committee
L&T	Learning and Teaching
LMS	Learning Management Systems
MASN	maximum aggregate student numbers
NDT	National Disability Team
NQF	National Qualifications Framework
OECD	Organisation for Economic Co-operation and Development
OSCD	Objective Structured Clinical Examination
PDP	Personal Development Planning
QA	quality assurance
QAA	Quality Assurance Agency
QCA	Qualifications and Curriculum Authority
QE	quality enhancement
RDN	Resource Delivery Network
SCQF	Scottish Credit and Qualifications Framework
SENDA	Special Educational Needs and Disability Act

SIMS	Student Information Management System
TASI	Technical Advisory Service for Images
VLE	Virtual Learning Environment
WP	Widening Participation

Chapter 1

The higher education context

INTRODUCTION

Your career interests and energies at the moment will probably be very much focused on your subject, your students, your school/department and possibly a little on the higher education institution (HEI) that you work in – which is what one would expect as you come to terms with the demands of your job/Ph.D. and start your teaching career. But what about the wider picture of higher education (HE): what do you know about it? What is going on out there that influences what you do? What has changed over the last 40 years that is having a major impact on the student experience today? What has changed since the time when you were an undergraduate? We ask you to think about these things as even though they may seem a little remote from where you are sitting, they do have a bearing on your students: the way they approach their studies, their hopes and beliefs about higher education, and their expectations of you.

To get you thinking, here are six questions about the wider context of HE:

1   How many students in total (undergraduate and postgraduate) are there in HEIs in your country?
2   What is the total annual income of all of the HEIs in your country?
3   Are there more men or more women in the total student population in your country?
4   What is the ratio of full-time to part-time undergraduate students in your country?

5 How many jobs are there in your country for you as an academic in an HEI?

6 What, across the sector in your country, is the average staff to student ratio?

We are not going to give exact answers to any of these questions because, of course, they will change the day after this book is published and we are not sure which country you work in. However, in the notes at the end of this chapter, there are approximate answers for the UK at the end of 2005. The place to find all the current data in the UK is the Higher Education Statistics Agency (HESA) at www.hesa.ac.uk and all numerical information included in this chapter has been derived from figures available from them.

This chapter will consider some of the factors that are influencing higher education today, and how things have changed over the last few decades. Many of these issues are common across higher education in the developed nations. As we are more familiar with the UK, we have chosen to use it as our case study to discuss and illustrate the issues. Readers outside the UK will have to consult local data and statistics for comparison, and we have included some reference points at the end of this chapter. This information should help you to put things into context, and it should also give you an insight into the perspectives of HE and students that some of your colleagues might hold. The topics we will discuss, which we do not claim to be comprehensive but should give you a flavour, are:

- increasing student numbers
- widening participation
- life-long learning
- disability equality duty
- internationalisation of the curriculum
- research-informed teaching
- quality assurance
- the impact of C&IT.

The first four in the list are closely interrelated and will be considered together. We will discuss the others under separate headings, but they all impinge on the **quality of the student experience**, which is the unifying theme of this chapter.

THE GROWTH IN NUMBERS ATTENDING HE IN THE UK

If you talk to someone who graduated in the late 1960s or early 1970s – a fifty-something – it is likely that they will have been to university at a time when only about 6 per cent of school leavers did so. Their fellow students would have been mostly full-time, of school-leaving age and most would have been from the UK. In the mid-sixties the total student population in the UK was about 400,000, rising to nearly 600,000 in the early seventies. This compares with a total student population of around 2,100,000 in 2004/2005 – a fivefold increase in 40 years. For that mid-sixties/early seventies cohort of students, it is very likely that being full-time meant just that, in that it is less likely that they worked in term-time as their university costs were paid and they received a reasonable means-tested, state allowance (a student grant) to cover living costs. Some might describe this as the heyday for being a student!

A graduate from the late 1980s/early 1990s – a thirty-something – is likely to describe a very different experience. Numbers in higher education rose very rapidly between 1987 and 1993, particularly in the polytechnic and HE college sectors. Jary and Jones (2004) among others have described this as a shift from an elite to a mass-education system, and they provide a useful review of the impact of the increase. At the same time, government spending on education did not rise appreciably and the staff–student ratio worsened considerably. But at least student grants, to some extent, were still available.

Students who have attended university over the last five to ten years – a twenty-something, which of course could include you – have yet another tale to tell and this one is rather more woeful than others. While student numbers did not change dramatically during that period, a major reduction in monetary support for students saw a shift in how higher education was paid for: more was paid by the students (and/or their families) and less by the state. The introduction of top-up fees and student loans has resulted in more, so-called, full-time students working during term-time. The adverse impact of this on achievement was reported in a 'Survey of higher education students' attitudes to debt and term-time working and their impact on attainment' (HEFCE, 2005a) which was published in November 2005. Two telling quotes from the report illustrate the impact:

Term-time working is associated with lower degree classifications and the more hours that students work the greater the likelihood of getting a poor degree [p. 113].

For a student working 16 hours a week (the average number of hours worked by those who do paid-work [p. 77]) the odds of getting a good degree to not getting a good degree are about 60 per cent the odds for a similar non-working student [p. 117].

The survey reported that slightly more than half of the students who were canvassed had paid employment during term-time at some stage in their final two years of undergraduate study. There are a number of social and ethnic variations in the figures that give rise to concern and need to be addressed. In addition to student loans and fees changing students' attitudes to debt (it was viewed as a normal part of today's lifestyle), they have raised the expectation of a well-paid job being a product of HE and hence what higher education and the curriculum are all about. Using a range of technologies to support teaching and learning, as will be discussed throughout this book, can help to alleviate some of the problems that arise for students juggling study and finances, as well as providing a better experience and service for all students.

Figure 1.1 shows that the growth in student numbers levelled out in the late 1990s as some restrictions were placed on HEIs. An era of

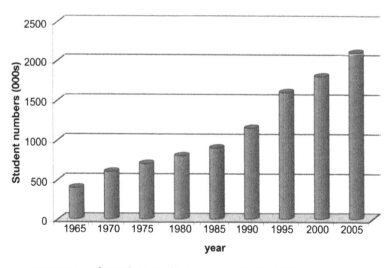

FIGURE 1.1 Growth in student numbers in the UK

'maximum aggregate student numbers' (MASN) existed when boundaries on the growth in numbers of home students were enforced by the government. The rules of enforcement were simple – an institution could exceed the number of students that was allocated to it, but it would not receive funding for the extra students. That tended to keep most in check. During that period, the opportunities for growth in HEIs came from the major increase in the international student market, to which we will return later. Since 2000/2001 there have been a variety of schemes to increase the number of home students in HE, but the emphasis has been on representation from **all** groups within society, and these have extended in the light of the UK government's target of 50 per cent participation by 2010. The Higher Education Funding Council for England (HEFCE, 2005b) sums up the initiatives well:

> all those with the potential to benefit from higher education have the opportunity to do so, whatever their background and whenever they need it. This means providing for the needs of a growing number of students with a broad variety of previous life and educational experiences. These students may return on more than one occasion across their lifetime in order to refresh their knowledge, upgrade their skills and sustain their employability.

There are two important strands in the HEFCE statement: **potential to benefit** and **return on more than one occasion**. The first requires that higher education is made more accessible, and this aspect has been addressed in part by widening participation initiatives and in part by Special Educational Needs and Disability Act (SENDA) legislation, now updated by the Disability Discrimination Bill. The second aspect – **return on more than one occasion** – has shifted the focus from HE as a one-time opportunity, usually the initiator of a life-time career, to a possible multi-stage process to allow updating and reskilling as required; we have moved into the era of lifelong learning. The following three sections deal with each of these aspects in turn.

Widening Participation (WP)

Research has shown that the increase in student numbers in the UK that was reported earlier was not representative of all social classes. Disproportionately more of the three higher social classes (I, II and IIIN) attended university compared to the three lower classes (IIIM, IV

5

and V). Many see this as an 'aspiration' problem. Fewer young people from the three lower social groups see university as a place for them, and those who do aim for HE tend to set their sights lower and take places in the less prestigious universities, even though their entry qualifications would open most doors.

Many of the schemes that have been established by institutions to address the WP challenge have focused on this aspect of aspiration and have resulted in work with pupils of all ages in schools. The aim is to increase the number of applicants from all social groups. Other initiatives have looked at ways in which WP students can be supported once they have entered higher education, the focus being on retention rather than admissions. The term **non-traditional student** is useful here as it reminds us that the systems and support mechanisms that generally are in place have proved appropriate for students with a different set of qualifications, life experiences, aspirations and expectations. We cannot expect such systems to cope with very different demands, and additional and more diverse structures need to be provided. This has resulted in the strengthening of some aspects of support that already existed within institutions, particularly skills development, as well as the addition of extra support, such as attendance tracking. Details of a range of other ideas and mechanisms for both increasing applications and assisting retention can be obtained under the widening participation tag at the HEFCE website www.hefce.ac.uk.

DISABILITY EQUALITY DUTY (DED)

In April 2005, the Disability Discrimination Act, DDA (2005), was passed by the UK Government. This new legislation amends and extends the existing provision under the DDA (1995) and builds on the Special Educational Needs and Disability Act, SENDA (2001). SENDA set the framework and direction for the new legislation by requiring for the first time that HEIs make reasonable adjustments to ensure that disabled people are not put at a substantial disadvantage in relation to people who are not disabled in accessing HE, and that these adjustments should be anticipatory rather than in reaction to a need.

The new legislation goes even further by placing a Disability Equality Duty (DED) on public bodies which means that, from December 2006, HEIs are required to promote equality of opportunity and positive attitudes towards disabled people (including staff, students and visitors), even if that means treating them more favourably. This means that insti-

6

tutions (and their staff) must take a proactive approach and mainstream disability equality into everything they do – policy/decision-making and activities. The Disability Rights Commission has produced a Code of Practice that sets out what this means in practice (see www.drc-gb.org) and provides examples of both the general and specific duties institutions are required to undertake. Although we have tried to summarise the legislation and its implications, the code is some 35,000 words, so you can see the need for finding out a little more about how this legislation is being addressed in your own institution. And, given that in the UK just over 6 per cent of the full-time students who returned disability information on their application forms recorded some type of disability, this means that in most groups of students you teach, there is some form of special educational need that legislation requires must be addressed.

The term 'disabled' has a broad definition and can include people with:

- physical impairments, some of which may restrict mobility;
- hearing – reduced/restricted/deaf;
- visual – minor/restricted/blind;
- dyslexia – a specific learning difficulty in the acquisition of reading, writing and spelling, and is neurological in origin;
- other conditions that impair ability to learn in a particular manner;
- mental health conditions;
- HIV, cancer or multiple sclerosis from the point of diagnosis;
- general health problems.

You must realise that it is not your individual responsibility to deal with these issues; rather, it is the institution as a whole, including the teaching staff, who must respond in order to make reasonable adjustments and avoid less favourable treatment. You are part of a team in this matter and must be aware of what is in place and your part in this.

Lifelong learning

The number of people who return to study to extend their qualifications base is increasing. The term **lifelong learning** is often used to describe this trend, and returning students have become a major group within our institutions. Many of these students, through necessity or choice, are part-time. At the time of writing, about 17 per cent of all first-degree students in the UK are part-timers, while over 57 per cent of postgraduate students are part-time. In addition, many are 'mature', which in HE statistics speak is aged 21 or over. In 2004/2005 over 50 per cent of all first-year undergraduates in the UK were 'mature'. Life-long learners are returning to education to extend and build on their qualifications – Bachelors to Masters; HND to Bachelors; life and work experience to qualifications – and so refresh their knowledge, understanding and skills. They are, of course, bringing a very different educational and experiential background from those who transfer directly from courses in schools or colleges.

You may wonder why we have included this information. We reply with several questions, all of which have a yes/no answer, but which also require your reasoning:

- Do you think that the approaches to learning that part-time students adopt to their studies will differ from those of full-timers?
- Does age matter in terms of approaches to learning?
- Do you think that the targets, motivators and skills of students directly from school differ from those of mature students with less formal qualifications but a wealth of work/life experience?
- Given the possible heterogeneous mix that will be in your classes in terms of age, previous educational background, possibly part/full time (depending on how the course is arranged), students with disabilities and, as we will mention later, ethnic mix and international students, do you see heterogeneity in the class as a disadvantage ?

As before, we do not plan to answer these questions in detail here, but believe that you will gain a useful overview and insight both from the remainder of this book and many of the resources that we include at the end of the chapters. And, while on the subject of student learning, don't forget the website that is associated with this series: www.routledge falmer.com/series/KGETHE/.

In summary to this section, we have suggested that the increasing size of the student population has brought with it a number of challenges as well as benefits. In order to maintain the quality of the student experience, we suggest that you need to find out what is happening within your own institution about these topics, and that you discover as much as you can about your own student groups and the ways in which you might need to support them. We expect that the outcome of this will be that you will have to adjust your expectations and assumptions about what your students already know, can do, expect to gain from higher education and how they see your role in the process.

INTERNATIONALISING THE CURRICULUM

As noted above, the growth in student numbers in the UK has been both in the home (which includes the EU) and the international market. Nearly 30 per cent of all postgraduate students in UK HEIs are from outside the EU. This means that we have a diverse and rich resource to work with. Yet many of our courses, in terms of the topics studied and the examples used, are not only UK-centric but many are also locally based. We do not open our students' eyes to the wider vistas and expect them to think in a global way. The need is, therefore, to make our courses more outward looking – to internationalise the curriculum.

What does internationalising the curriculum mean and how is it done?

Internationalisation certainly does mean ensuring that all students understand the international context of their discipline or professional course, that the content of their course incorporates multinational experience and thought, and that ideally they have the opportunity to study a portion of their course in another country. International-isation also means that the way in which the course is delivered is culturally inclusive.

(Robinson, 2000)

In unpicking this definition, there are several possible strands to inter-nationalising the curriculum (NSW, 2002):

■ the curriculum should include international matters and issues;
■ students should be encouraged to think nationally, internationally and globally;
■ the institution as a whole should make a distinctive international contribution.

The various aspects could be achieved through a number of interrelated initiatives (Monash, 2001) that target different aspects of the teaching and learning process.

9

For staff:

- establish and support international exchange programmes/study leave/collaboration in both research and teaching, and ensure that there is spin-off in both;
- increase international recruitment and maintain links with international alumni;
- incorporate international perspectives in teaching materials, examples and literature;
- share good practice in capitalising on student diversity in the teaching and learning process.

For students:

- encourage participation in study abroad/exchange programmes through guidance and scholarships;
- involve students in supporting the diverse student population within the school/faculty;
- review induction programmes for appropriateness in terms of multicultural and multiethnic ethos;
- introduce/extend cross-cultural student mentoring/proctoring initiatives;
- encourage extra-curricular activities that focus on relevant commercial/international topics.

For the curriculum:

- introduce a comparative or international focus in appropriate aspects of programmes and subjects;
- purchase or produce teaching materials that have an international focus;
- promote foreign language/culture modules as electives or options within courses;
- ensure administration and support processes throughout the student life-cycle are culturally inclusive, and accommodate the expectations and requirements of all students.

For the university:

- create links with international companies and institutions;
- review the outward face of the school/faculty and reposition accordingly – this might be as simple as reviewing publicity materials;

- establish networks with international alumni;
- establish bilateral institutional links abroad to enable academic and research collaboration and student exchange.

We hope that these ideas have provoked you to start thinking about the local/national/international/global dimensions and their balance within your teaching, the examples you use, the materials you provide for students, and the literature and resources you recommend to students.

THE TEACHING–RESEARCH RELATIONSHIP

If we ask the question 'what makes higher education different from earlier stages of education (secondary and further)?' the answer must be research: the focus on creating and discovering as well as disseminating knowledge. It follows, therefore, that our teaching (as a form of dissemination) should have this added value of being linked to creation and discovery – i.e. it should be research-informed. But how is teaching in universities informed by research? Griffiths (2004) developed a typology of teaching–research links: research-led, research-oriented, research-based and research-informed. These are useful ways to consider the notion of linking teaching and research.

Typical scenarios that we see frequently and that map reasonably well on to the Griffiths typology are:

- Teaching staff incorporate current research into their teaching as case studies and examples. Aspects of courses, final year in particular, are based on the current research of members of staff. It is the outcomes of research that is important in this instance.
- Students are taught and practise 'research skills' as part of the course – the focus here is the process rather than the outcome of research, and the skills can be library as well as laboratory based. In addition, students may engage in the research process themselves in various ways: final year projects and dissertations; students working with university staff or on placements with colleagues who are researching.
- The method of teaching is enquiry based – the students engage with the content in response to problems and issues that they are required to resolve. Throughout the curriculum, the students learn by researching the subject, rather than episodically researching the content, as in the example above.

- Staff engage in research into pedagogy that informs the design of the curriculum and the learning and teaching process. This may be as part of the postgraduate certificate or diploma course that they register for as part of their initial training or continuing professional development.

While you may be taking a postgraduate certificate or equivalent course as part of your initial development, it is important that you think about the ways in which the students connect with research – the outcomes as well as the process – in your discipline. How will you integrate research into your teaching and the students' learning experience?

QUALITY ASSURANCE

As we note in Chapter 2, if you refer to course design models described in recent books, evaluation and review will figure large. Prior to 1990, certainly in the UK, this would have been less of an issue. Of course, educational provision was reviewed, refined and refreshed, but the initiative and drivers for this were more likely to be personal than institutional, and the frequency was more opportunistic than periodic and regular. The early 1990s saw a dramatic change in the quality assurance arena, and the era of review, audit and inspection dawned.

First on the UK national scene was the Higher Education Quality Council, and this was followed by the Quality Assurance Agency (QAA) which continues, in a different format and role, today (see www.qaa. ac.uk). The process and focus of quality assurance initiatives has shifted over time as experience has informed practice and institutional methods have matured. The following potted history gives the flavour rather than the specifics of this evolution.

Originally, external review in order to assure the quality of provision and the processes governing the provision was at both institutional and subject level: audit and subject review. At institutional level, the questions were at the process and procedures level:

- How are standards moderated and maintained in the institution?
- What processes exist to monitor and measure the quality of individual courses?
- How is support for students – academic and pastoral – provided across the campus and how is equality of provision assured for all students?

These were the big questions about the business of awarding degrees, whereas at the subject level, the detail was more important:

- What is the course trying to achieve?
- Does it achieve its aims?
- How do you know?
- How do you support learners?
- What is the resource base?

Over time (1993–2002), all subjects were reviewed by a process of peer review. All institutions were invited to nominate staff members to act as reviewers, and those selected were trained in the process. From this cohort, cross-institutional teams from the subject area were formed and they carried out the reviews. The methodology changed over the period, but the primary purpose – assessing quality and quality assurance mechanisms – remained. The last round of subject reviews was based on a fairly simple framework that, if slightly elaborated, provides a useful course design tool.

The process began with the question 'What are you trying to achieve?'. This was asking what the aims and outcomes of the course were: a description of what a graduate should know and be able to do as a result of their studies. Based on the answer, the following six aspects were researched:

How the claimed aims and outcomes were achieved by:

1 the design, content and organisation of the curriculum;
2 the teaching, learning and assessment methods being used;
3 the student support and guidance measures in place;
4 the resources that are provided;
5 the ways in which the course is reviewed and renewed – the quality assurance (QA) and quality enhancement (QE) arrangements;

and what evidence there was of achievement of these claims:

6 in the facts and figures of student achievement and progression.

While most colleagues would probably agree that, as professional educators, the questions being asked were reasonable, many were unhappy with the process of obtaining the answers. The procedures became

13

heavily bureaucratic, and huge amounts of time and paper were expended. The result of reviews was a report that was a useful snapshot and perception of practice, but it was accompanied by grades or scores. Early on in the process, an overall grade of satisfactory, good or excellent was awarded, and later the six aspects were scored on a 1–4 (top) basis. Not surprisingly, but inappropriately, these six scores were summed to give a score out of 24 and league tables were based around the numbers.

There are two important points to be aware of from the subject review process. First, while all subjects were reviewed over a period of years, each subject only happened once. As a result, subject areas within your institution are still labelled with the grades/scores that were awarded in that single round and have not had an opportunity to redeem or consolidate. The fact that the methodology changed over the period makes comparisons even less meaningful. Second, the reports that were written are available on the QAA website, and summaries of the provision and examples of good practice were produced. It might be worth checking, therefore, on the report for your area and the summary.

Other parts of the world have engaged in similar moves to measure the quality provision, but using very different means. Australia, for example, has used the Course Evaluation Questionnaire (CEQ), which is completed by students at graduation. In this instance, the measure is of student satisfaction at the end of a course, and gives a view of both subject and institution. This approach has informed the development of the National Student Survey in the UK, which was introduced in academic year 2004/2005 and polls the opinions of students in the final term of their final year on a number of issues (www.hefce.ac.uk/learning/iss/). The results are published and form the basis of yet more league tables. It will be interesting to see how, and if, the methodology develops.

As a result of a little over a decade of external audit and review in the UK, the sector has matured considerably in its approach to quality assurance. In general, the outcomes have been positive and HE was shown to be relatively 'healthy'. The process has now shifted from one of external to internal review: institutional autonomy for quality assurance has been acknowledged. In some parts of the UK, external review continues at institutional level and is designed to establish levels of confidence in the procedures that institutions have in place to monitor standards and assure the quality of their courses. In addition, the following external reference points – termed academic infrastructure – must be taken into account by institutions:

- subject benchmark statements;
- code of practice for the assurance of academic quality and standards in higher education;
- framework for higher education qualification;
- Programme Specifications.

Each of these will be discussed in appropriate parts of this book.

Many who work in staff and educational development have been very supportive of the subject review process as it has shone lights in places that had not been visited before; there was much gain from the pain. However, the pain cannot be denied. The move to more local – institutional – accountability has reduced the intensity and publicity of review, but hopefully will retain the robustness and value of the process.

Scotland has moved more to a focus on quality enhancement and, through a series of funded initiatives, is attempting to raise standards and develop practice (see www.qaa.ac.uk/scotland). The variations that we have illustrated above cause us to remind you to find out the processes that operate both at national, institutional and local level for you, and to be aware of the impact on the work you do with your students.

IMPACT OF C&IT

The last ten years has seen a rise in the use of computer technology in teaching, not only in higher education, but also in schools, colleges and workplace learning. The expansion and development of the World Wide Web (Web) has touched all parts of our lives: we access information and services in new ways and communicate (instantly) with people we may never meet. In the UK, there have been a number of national initiatives to encourage teachers to embrace the use of new technologies to support and manage their teaching. In 2005, the Government Department for Education and Skills published the e-strategy 'Harnessing Technology: Transforming Learning and Children's Services' to encourage teachers in schools to make appropriate use of e-learning (www.dfes.gov.uk/). In the same year, HEFCE published their own strategy for the next ten years (www.hefce.ac.uk/). It states:

People use the internet and new technologies every day – for finding information, communicating, and seeking entertainment, goods and services. Learners are bringing new expectations of the power of technology into higher education. And the curiosity and innovation of those in higher education is driving them to explore new approaches to learning supported by technologies. It is the excitement and interest of learners, teachers and the sector in general that drives our e-learning strategy. Our goal is to help the sector use new technology as effectively as they can, so that it becomes a 'normal' or embedded part of their activities.

(HEFCE, 2005c, Foreword)

Similar policies can also be found for higher education in other countries – for example, Australia www.education.gov.au/goved/. In the UK, the Association for Learning Technology (ALT, www.alt.ac.uk/) provides a journal and annual conference for staff in higher education to showcase their work. One of the largest organisations in the UK with regard to C&IT in learning and teaching is the Joint Information Systems Committee (JISC, www.jisc.ac.uk/). JISC provide advice and guidance to institutions about procedures and systems that can be used to further e-learning. Another book in this series, *Using C&IT to Support Teaching*, looks in detail at the use of C&IT in teaching. It is clear that technology, and particularly the Web, play a large part in the tools and techniques for designing learning.

From this very broad picture of HE and the range of external influences, we move on to the design of teaching and learning. First, we will look at a number of design models and then progress to a detailed discussion of each aspect of the design process.

 NOTES

For the UK in 2005/2006, the answers to the six questions on pp. 1–2 are:

1   Just over two million – 2,100,000 in 2005.
2   £17 billion.
3   More women than men in the total student population – 56 per cent to 44 per cent in 2005. Women overtook men as a proportion of undergraduates in 1996/1997.
4   About 5 to 1.
5   About 150,000 academic jobs in the 146 HEIs.
6   The average staff to student ratio is 1:18.

FURTHER RESOURCES

Quality assurance

The European Association for Quality Assurance in Higher Education, which gives links to all Quality Agencies for HE in Europe: www.enqa/net/index.lasso

The Australian Universities Quality Agency: www.auqa.edu.au/

Council for Higher Education Accreditation in the USA: www.chea.org/

International Network for Quality Assurance Agencies in Higher Education: www.inqaahe.org/

New Zealand Universities Academic Audit Unit: www.aau.ac.nz/

Quality assurance at Canada's universities: www.aucc.ca/qa/index_e.html

WP

A very useful source of information about WP initiatives (WP A–Z) can be found on the HEFCE site at www.hefce.ac.uk/widen/a_z.asp

Research-informed teaching

Institutional strategies to link teaching and research. Alan Jenkins and Mick Healey. HE Academy: www.heacademy.ac.uk/resources.asp?process=full_record&section=generic&id=585. Accessed 5 December 2005.

The third issue of *Exchange* was published in December 2002. Its focus was on linking research and teaching: Mick Healey and Alan Jenkins were the guest editors. www.exchange.ac.uk/issue3.asp

Disciplinary case studies on teaching/research links. Produced by Heather Sears as part of the Subject Centre Bioscience contribution to Linking Teaching and Research in the Disciplines. Available at www.bioscience.heacademy.ac.uk/projects/ltr/. Accessed 21 December 2005.

Statistics

UK – The Higher Education Statistics Agency (HESA): www.hesa.ac.uk

Australia – statistics available at www.dest.gov.au/sectors/higher_education/publications_resources/statistics/default.htm

C&IT

ALT is a professional and scholarly association that seeks to bring together all those with an interest in the use of learning technology: www.alt.ac.uk/

The Joint Information Systems Committee (JISC) UK: www.jisc.ac.uk/

Funding

Higher Education Funding – international comparison: www.dfes.gov.uk/ hegateway/uploads/HEfunding_internationalcomparison.pdf. Thirteen OECD (Organisation for Economic Co-operation and Development) member countries are compared.

Chapter 2

How your teaching fits into the bigger picture

INTRODUCTION

While, currently, you may not be responsible for designing any large parts of the curriculum, it is important to understand how your part in the teaching process links to all other aspects of the students' learning experience. In other words, how your teaching fits within the module, the level, the programme, the department, the university and beyond. To achieve this, you need to be aware of the basics of curriculum design and some of the models in use.

Biggs (1999) reminds us that alignment in the curriculum is important, and Entwistle (2005) gives a similar message of curriculum coherence (the latter descriptor being seen as less linear than the former). But what does alignment/coherence in curriculum terms mean and how does it impact on the work that you will do with your students?

To answer this we need to think about:

■   value added
■   fitness for purpose
■   fitness of purpose.

This may sound like management speak, but these are three very useful measures to consider.

Value added, fitness for purpose and fitness of purpose

The three terms are important across the complete spectrum of design, whether we are talking about the whole curriculum or a single session (lecture, tutorial, practical session in a laboratory, etc.).

Value added

What will the students gain as a result of their learning? What will they know, be able to do, how will their thinking and behaviour change as a result of the teaching/learning experience? Obviously, this depends on what they know at the onset (which is a vital question for any course design process), and what the purpose of the learning is (the intended learning outcomes – see Chapter 3). Value added is the gain as a result of the process.

As teachers, we cannot guarantee that our plans for students' learning (intended learning) will take place. In the same way, we cannot control what other learning (unintended learning) will occur. All we can do is be clear about the proposed learning and provide a quality teaching/learning opportunity supported by the appropriate resources. In addition, we need to inform our students of what they could gain by taking full advantage of the learning episodes in the curriculum. It is one of the teacher's responsibilities to inform students of the course's plans and opportunities, and to assist them to reflect on their learning.

Fitness for purpose

Is the intended learning appropriate for the students in the group? This does not only link to their previous learning, but also their level, abilities and needs. We will talk more about level later in this chapter. Also, are the appropriate resources available (library, computing, access to staff and time)? What value is there to life beyond the course (employability/enterprise skills – see Chapter 6)?

Fitness of purpose

Is the work appropriate to the standards and expectations of the qualification that the students are studying for? This is another vital question for any course design process. What is the level/demand of the work? Is it appropriate? One of the most common questions/concerns of colleagues starting their career is how they should pitch their teaching at the correct level.

COURSE DESIGN MODELS, LEVEL DESCRIPTORS AND BENCHMARK STATEMENTS

To set a context to allow us to consider and answer the issues and topics raised above, it will be useful to:

- consider one course design model in detail and refer to several others;
- start to understand and use level descriptors;
- be aware of the benchmark statements that exist for most undergraduate, and a few taught postgraduate, courses.

All of these topics are invaluable to our planning.

Course design and review models

Newble and Canon (1989) summarised the task of successful course design neatly by stating that the key is 'to forge educationally sound and logical links between planned intentions, course content, teaching and learning methods, and the assessment of student learning while taking full account of student characteristics'.

Note the emphasis on the alignment/coherence that was mentioned earlier. There are various cycles, models and schemas that have been proposed to assist us to achieve this. The one used throughout this book is shown in Figure 2.1 below (Dennis, 1990). This cycle is particularly useful because:

- it is **cyclic**, and so emphasises that changing one aspect has an impact on other parts of the cycle and that it is necessary to review all of the component parts and not just some of them;
- it is **comprehensive**, if you take account of all of the aspects there is nothing left to chance;
- it **ensures coherence**, as all of the components in the cycle are linked;
- it reminds us that the course design process is **iterative**, as all the arrows go both ways and all the aspects are linked;
- it can be used both as a course **design** tool **and** as a course **review** process.

You will notice that the model emphasises the importance of aims and learning outcomes (see Chapter 3) by placing them at the apex: we must be clear of the intentions of the courses that we offer. Based on these, we can select the content (see Chapter 4) that will enable our students to achieve the intentions. We believe that teachers should work from outcomes to content rather than the reverse. (There is another design model that places content as central, with all other aspects radiating from this – see Figure 2.2). Based on the outcomes and the content,

21

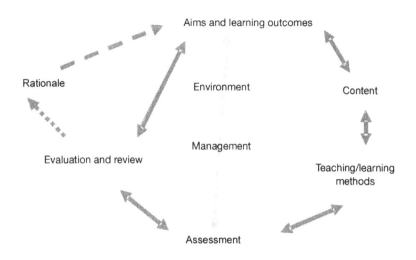

Aims and learning outcomes

Rationale

Environment

Content

Evaluation and review

Management

Teaching/learning
methods

Assessment

FIGURE 2.1 Course design and review model

we can think about the approaches to learning and teaching, how we can best sequence topics, the time that will be spent on the various topics and how we group the students (see Chapter 5). Of course, life is not so linear, as the last few sentences suggest: restrictions on methods could link back to content etc. So we need to optimise the curriculum by taking an iterative approach in order to take account of all the opportunities and restrictions. But there is one part of the cycle that must have a direct link – between outcomes and assessment (see Chapter 6). The assessment process must be designed to test the intended learning, to find out what students are able to do, rather than what they cannot.

Following the cycle round, the next component is evaluation and review – to check whether what is on offer is fit for its purpose (see Chapter 10). We are not, however, restricted to checking whether the standard of teaching was acceptable, but should also be measuring the appropriateness and quality of the resources, and whether the curriculum is current, relevant and at an appropriate level. This requires that we consult a range of reviewers and not just students. Students can provide vital information about our courses, but there are some things that they are not able to tell us. The environment and management aspects hover, helicopter-like, above (and below) the whole cycle.

The environment aspect incorporates student support (academic and pastoral support), provision of resources and establishing the 'learning community', which involves achieving the right conditions for both challenging and supporting our students (see Chapters 7 and 8). The management aspect ensures that we have thought clearly about the lines of responsibility and provision of information. Management here includes the full spectrum from the top level (planning and developing), through to the day-to-day operational (ensuring there are enough chairs in the correct room at the appropriate time), and includes responding and reacting to issues as they arise (see Chapter 9).

Last in our quick tour of this model comes rationale. The dotted lines are not supposed to devalue its significance; rather, they remind us that while this aspect is vital when the course is being established (course design), rationale only needs to be revisited or reflected on occasionally. However, the remainder of the cycle needs to be continually reviewed and monitored (course review).

If your preference is for words, rather than diagrams, the same cycle can be resolved into a series of questions, as shown in Table 2.1.

In summary, Figure 2.1 provides an overview of course design and review. It shows the links and emphasises the need for coherence within the curriculum. And, as noted above, later chapters in the book deal separately with each aspect in some detail (except rationale). You should hold the model in mind when reading the separate chapters in order to remind yourself of the interconnections. As we will not revisit the rationale aspect of course design elsewhere in this book, we need to deal with it in this chapter.

TABLE 2.1 Course design and review questions

Design cycle	Design question
Rationale	Why are we doing this?
Aims and learning outcomes	What should the learners be able to do?
Content	What content will be needed to achieve it?
Teaching/learning methods	How are we planning to enable it?
Assessment	How will we know that the learners have achieved the goals?
Environment	What support will the learners need?
Management	How will we make it happen?
Evaluation and review	How might it be improved?
Rationale	Is this still valid?

Rationale

When establishing a new course, there are a number of questions, not in any priority order, that must be considered:

- What will the course add to the existing provision?
- How does it fit the school/department mission?
- Who are the target group for the course?
- Who will teach and support the course?
- Is there a market for the course/who will register for it?
- What is the business plan?
- Is there a job market for the graduates of the course?
- Is there similar provision elsewhere/what makes this proposal stand out?
- What are the resource issues: library, IT, equipment and space?

As you can see, most of these questions are about income and expenditure – the sustainability of the course rather than the educational merit. But the bottom line is that any course has to be marketable to students and to prospective employers of the students, and must generate sufficient funding to make it viable.

Other course design/review models

There are a few other design models that you might wish to consider. We have already mentioned the idea of content being central to the

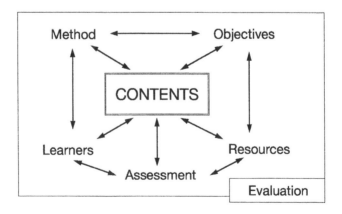

FIGURE 2.2 Morale C

design process and the Brown (1995) model does just that. The design model shown in Figure 2.2 is based on the earlier Moral C approach, but has been extended to add the essential component of evaluation. The Moral C name of the model was based on the first letters of the original components – **m**ethods, **o**bjectives, **r**esources, etc. To be current, we have renamed it Morale C, and have included it here because it has content at its centre, which is different from the cycle shown in Figure 2.1. In addition, it could easily be used as a checklist for designing a single session, as well as looking at a larger chunk of the curriculum.

The notion of a focus for curriculum planning is extended by Harden (1986/1998). He briefly discusses the values and pitfalls of a range of approaches to, or perspectives on, planning, some of which are listed below:

- Engineering approach: here the emphasis is on specifying the curriculum through the aims and outcomes.
- Mechanic's approach: the 'mechanics of the method of instruction – teaching methods and techniques – are of paramount importance'.
- Cookbook approach: the content (ingredients) of the curriculum is to the fore.
- Railway approach: this focuses on timetables and ordering of the curriculum.
- Detective approach: evaluates the curriculum (and puts right the problems that are encountered).
- Religious approach: a particular belief, perhaps in the efficacy of a particular mode of instruction, dominates the curriculum.
- Bureaucratic approach: norms, rules and regulations mould the curriculum.

A particular value of this list is that it reinforces the need to look at curriculum planning from a range of perspectives in order to give a coherent, aligned and inclusive outcome.

Another curriculum design model that we recommend you look at was proposed by Moon (2002): the basic map of module development. We particularly like a number of features of her model:

- it is **cyclic** – emphasising the links and knock-on effects of any change as discussed above;

- it reminds us to think carefully about the **level** of study – a point we will discuss below;
- it contains a very useful triangle linking outcomes, assessment method and threshold assessment criteria;
- it contains an explicit statement that makes one reconsider what is planned – it contains an **iterative** stage.

The last model is less of a model and more of a directive: constructive alignment of the curriculum. This was put forward by John Biggs (1999) and has dominated writing on course design in recent years. He emphasised the need to relate **curriculum objectives** with **teaching/learning activities** and **assessment tasks**. You will come across other models and they say much the same. The differences tend to be of emphasis rather than content, and some take a wider view of the design process and so include more aspects.

In addition to these various models, there are two checklists that we recommend you take account of when planning your teaching. The first is from Harden (1986/1999) and is a list of ten questions that he suggests you ask during planning; the questions have a number of synergies with the model that we propose. His focus was medical curricula, which explains the first, pragmatic, question. However, in the light of fitness for purpose that was discussed earlier, this is an important question.

1   What are the needs in relation to the product of the training programme?
2   What are the aims and objectives?
3   What content should be included?
4   How should the content be organised?
5   What educational strategies should be adopted?
6   What teaching methods should be used?
7   How should assessment be carried out?
8   How should details of the curriculum be communicated?
9   What educational environment or climate should be fostered?
10   How should the process be managed?

The other checklist comes from Chickering and Gamson (1987) who suggested that good practice in undergraduate education includes the following seven principles:

1   Encourages contact between students and faculty, especially contact focused on the academic agenda.
2   Develops reciprocity and cooperation among students, teaching them to work productively with others.
3   Encourages active learning: doing and thinking about what they are doing.
4   Gives prompt feedback and helps students to figure out what to do in response.
5   Emphasises time on task: provides lots of useful, productive, guided practice.
6   Communicates high expectations and encourages students to have high self-expectations.
7   Respects diverse talents and ways of learning, and engenders respect for intellectual diversity.

We suggest that you select from all the above models and lists those aspects that seem to fit with your discipline and context. However, we strongly recommend that you retain the Dennis model shown in Figure 2.1 as this will remind you of all of the points that you need to take into account, and of the need for coherence and congruence.

Levels and level-descriptors

Ensuring progression is an important element of any curriculum design process: increasing the demand, complexity and uncertainty as students move through the course. Typically, an undergraduate programme comprises three years of study (exempting medicine and dentistry, and those that include a work or study placement either at home or abroad). Essential aids to think through the differences between the years are the level statements in the frameworks for higher education qualifications. The framework for England, Wales and Northern Ireland, published by the QAA (www.qaa.ac.uk) is called the Framework for Higher Education Qualifications (FHEQ), and this sits alongside the National Qualifications Framework (NQF, www.qca.org.uk). The framework for Scotland is an integral part of the wider Scottish Credit and Qualifications Framework (SCQF, www.scqf.org.uk/). Over the next few years these frameworks will be linked to a European standard that is currently being discussed; the initiative is called the Bologna Process. The aim is to establish a 'European Higher Education area' by 2010 (see www.dfes.gov.uk/bologna/ for more details). Two main purposes of the Bologna Process are to:

- enhance the mobility and employability of European citizens;
- increase the competitiveness of European HE.

Also, a European framework for qualifications will enable easy comparison of degrees and transfer of credits from one state to another.

Notice the distinction that is being made between the terms 'levels' and 'years'. The level describes the demand of the course, while the year refers to the chronological order in which students attend the course. It is not unknown for a mixed group of year 2 and year 3 students to attend the same level 2 or level 3 course. This may be a practical solution to a resource issue – the course can only be offered every other academic year due to staffing shortages or small numbers of students wishing to attend – rather than for a pedagogic reason. This could raise a number of pedagogic issues: for instance, do the year 2 students have the appropriate background and skills to access the level 3 course? Should year 2 and year 3 students be assessed in the same way, and against the same criteria? We will come back to these questions later.

It is, of course, essential to relate to the framework in force where you are located, but to provide examples for the discussion in this text we will refer to the Framework for Higher Education Qualifications (FHEQ) applicable to England, Wales and Northern Ireland (see Figure 2.3). This forms the top five levels of the nine-stage NQF that runs from entry level, through GCSE (levels 1 and 2) and A-levels (level 3) to undergraduate (levels 4–6), and finally postgraduate (levels 7 and 8) degrees.

Certificate	C level	Certificates of higher education
Intermediate	I level	Foundation degrees, ordinary (bachelors') degrees, diplomas of higher education and other higher diplomas
Honours	H level	Bachelors' degrees with honours, graduate certificates and graduate diplomas
Masters	M level	Masters' degrees, postgraduate certificates and postgraduate diplomas
Doctoral	D level	Doctorates

FIGURE 2.3 Framework for higher education qualifications

28

▓ TABLE 2.2 Level descriptors: honours

Honours degrees are awarded to students who have demonstrated:

(i)   a systematic understanding of key aspects of their field of study, including acquisition of coherent and detailed knowledge, at least some of which is at or informed by, the forefront of defined aspects of a discipline.

(ii) an ability to deploy accurately established techniques of analysis and enquiry within a discipline.

(iii) conceptual understanding that enables the student:

    (a) to devise and sustain arguments, and/or to solve problems, using ideas and techniques, some of which are at the forefront of a discipline, and

    (b) to describe and comment upon particular aspects of current research, or equivalent advanced scholarship, in the discipline.

(iv) an appreciation of the uncertainty, ambiguity and limits of knowledge.

(v)   the ability to manage their own learning, and to make use of scholarly reviews and primary sources (e.g. refereed research articles and/or original materials appropriate to the discipline).

Typically, holders of the qualification will be able to:

a   apply the methods and techniques that they have learned to review, consolidate, extend and apply their knowledge and understanding, and to initiate and carry out projects.

b   critically evaluate arguments, assumptions, abstract concepts and data (that may be incomplete), to make judgements, and to frame appropriate questions to achieve a solution – or identify a range of solutions – to a problem.

c   communicate information, ideas, problems and solutions to both specialist and non-specialist audiences.

and will have:

d   qualities and transferable skills necessary for employment requiring:

- the exercise of initiative and personal responsibility
- decision-making in complex and unpredictable contexts, and
- the learning ability needed to undertake appropriate further training of a professional or equivalent nature.

Source: QAA, 2001.

This is more than a ladder of success because, as you can see from the figure, the levels include a number of qualifications, and going deeper into the information provides descriptors of what students should, typically, be able to do at particular levels. In many ways, the comparison between levels is more useful than reading the individual levels. To start with, however, we will look at the descriptor for a qualification at honours (H) level taken (see Table 2.2).

29 ▓

TABLE 2.3 Comparison of level statements

Typically, holders of the qualification will be able to:

C – Certificate level	I – Intermediate level
Evaluate the appropriateness of different approaches to solving problems related to their area(s) of study and/or work	Use a range of established techniques to initiate and undertake critical analysis of information, and to propose solutions to problems arising from that analysis
Communicate the results of their study/work accurately and reliably, and with structured and coherent arguments	Effectively communicate information, arguments, and analysis, in a variety of forms, to specialist and non-specialist audiences, and deploy key techniques of the discipline effectively
Undertake further training and develop new skills within a structured and managed environment	Undertake further training, develop existing skills, and acquire new competences that will enable them to assume significant responsibility within organisations

Source: QAA, 2001.

The statements contained in the table give us a clear idea of what a typical graduate should be able to do, but not the level of sophistication, which is where the classification system fits in. But, more usefully for your purposes, let us compare the same aspects of the descriptors at two different levels, as in Table 2.3, remembering that the higher level assumes achievement of the lower.

Now we can see the difference in expectations at the various stages, and the learning outcomes set for your students should allow them, as a minimum, to achieve these different levels. In addition, you may find that your institution has produced a local version of the descriptors that better fit the context of your HEI. Whatever the case, it will be worth spending the hour or so that it takes to access and read the level C, I, H and M statements on the QAA website and think through their significance to your work with students.

It is also worth noting a small but important point caused by the alignment of qualifications to the FHEQ. To be awarded a particular qualification, a student must achieve the stated learning outcomes for that qualification. In the past, it might have been the case that a student who did not quite reach the honours level could be awarded an ordinary degree. This is no longer the case. To be awarded an honours degree, a student must achieve the honours degree outcomes at the honours degree level, and to gain an ordinary degree, the learning outcomes stated for that level must be achieved. This has meant that learning outcomes have had to be stated for all qualifications. You should find these details specified for the course that you teach in a document called the Programme Specification.

Programme Specification

As defined by the QAA (QAA, 1999a), a Programme Specification is 'a concise description of the intended outcomes of learning from a higher education programme, and the means by which these outcomes are achieved and demonstrated'. If this procedure is working well within your HEI, you should have access to documents that give learning outcomes and possibly guidance on content. It should provide you with information about the various components (modules) that make up the course and so tell you what else students are studying and what knowledge, skills and attributes they should be able to bring to your course. In addition, there should be some details about the ways in which the learning outcomes, at course level, are to be assessed, and the ways in which students will develop both subject-specific and more general (transferable) skills. The latter may be shown on a skills grid or matrix (see Chapter 4, p. 66). All this information will, by necessity, be outline, but it should help you to think through the options and possibilities when planning your classes.

An integral part of any undergraduate Programme Specification should be a link to the benchmark statement that the course takes account of. Like level descriptors, benchmark statements provide valuable context and guidance when planning a course. We will consider these in the final part of this section.

Subject benchmark statements

In recent years, the QAA has published 46 honours degree benchmark statements, the outcome of a major project designed to make explicit the general academic characteristics and standards of honours degrees in the UK. The QAA, working closely with a subject specialist in the sector, introduced the statements, and so we will use their definition (QAA,

2000a) to start our discussion of the use, and limitations, of this aspect of quality assurance of courses.

> Subject benchmark statements set out expectations about standards of degrees in a range of subject areas. They describe what gives a discipline its coherence and identity, and define what can be expected of a graduate in terms of the techniques and skills needed to develop understanding in the subject.

Table 2.4 lists the 46 statements for reference, so that you know what exists in your area and thus will have reason to read them. There are a number of other benchmark statements: a few for Masters degrees, several for NHS subjects, one for foundation degrees and some specifically for Scotland. Typically, the statements provide an overview of the subject-specific abilities, general intellectual skills and other key skills that a student studying a particular area should gain over the lifetime of their degree studies. As such, they set the scope of study for the qualification. In addition, some statements give descriptions of the quality of achievement that students might reach at threshold (pass) and modal (2:1 classification) levels.

Benchmark statements were not meant to establish a 'national curriculum' for each of the disciplines; and as you will see when you look at the statement for your subject, they are too general for that. Benchmark statements have a fine line to walk: if they are too detailed and specific they are criticised for trying to set a national curriculum and being burdensome; if they give too little detail, they are criticised for being too weak and woolly, and so open to interpretation that they are worthless. Despite these criticisms, they do give a very useful indication of the scope and qualities that should result from studying a discipline for employers, prospective students (and their parents who may well be funding the process) and staff new to teaching in higher education. But perhaps most importantly, the benchmark staements have made it clear, in all of the disciplines, that degrees are about more than subject content alone, and that all curricula must include both subject-specific and generic skills and approaches/attitudes.

Again, critics have said that degrees have always included these skills and attitudes, implicitly at least. We will not enter that debate here, but rather we will emphasise that the skills must be developed and suggest that making matters explicit is better than assuming that students recognise the implicit. It does not matter whether the skills and attitudes are

■ TABLE 2.4 Subject benchmark statements for undergraduate courses

Accounting	Agriculture, Forestry, Agricultural Sciences, Food Sciences and Consumer Sciences	Anthropology	Archaeology
Architecture, Architectural Technology and Landscape Architecture	Area Studies	Art and Design	Biomedical Science
Biosciences	Building and Surveying	Business and Management	Chemistry
Classics and Ancient History	Communication, Media, Film and Cultural Studies	Computing	Dance, Drama and Performance
Dentistry	Earth Science, Environmental Sciences and Environmental Studies	Economics	Education Studies
Engineering	English	Geography	Health Studies
History	History of Art, Architecture and Design	Hospitality, Leisure, Sport and Tourism	Languages and related subjects
Law	Librarianship and Information Management	Linguistics	Materials
Mathematics, Statistics and Operational Research	Medicine	Music	Optometry
Philosophy	Physics, Astronomy and Astrophysics	Politics and International Relations	Psychology
Social Policy and Administration and Social Work	Sociology	Theology and Religious Studies	Town and Country Planning
Veterinary Science	Welsh/Cymraeg		

Source: QAA, 2000a.

developed through particular 'skills' modules or units, or whether they are integrated within all modules (there are reasonably sound pedagogic and practical arguments for both approaches). What matters is that students are clear about the intended outcomes, and are encouraged and supported to reflect on their achievements, which is where personal development plans fit in (see Chapter 8).

Skills grids and maps

As benchmark statements have made clear the sorts of skills and attributes that should be developed (the 'what?'), the next course design questions are ones of 'how?' and 'when?'. This not only means whether we have the integrated or separate discussion noted above, but also at what stages/levels in the curriculum and at what points the skills are introduced, practised and assessed. You should find that a skills map for the course makes this clear. The value of a skills map is that our efforts can be better employed on progressing skills rather than on unnecessary repetition, and we will know what skills and attitudes we can assume, and build on, at the various stages of the degree course. A major, credit-bearing, team project should not be the place to initiate the learning of group and team skills. Rather, it should be the culmination of a series of opportunites, spread throughout the curriculum, for students to identify and practise the necessary skills. We will look at an example of a skills grid in Chapter 4 as one of a series of matrices/grids that can help us to build a coherent curriculum.

Before we move on to consider each aspect of the course design cycle, we need to consider four, final, general points: credits, curriculum shape, the QAA Code of Practice and VLEs.

CREDITS, SHAPES, QAA CODE OF PRACTICE AND VLES

Credits

How much work does a student have to do to obtain a degree? That is a bit like asking how long is a piece of string, but we do need to be able to put some notional idea of the typical number of hours that, normally, an average student should work in order to achieve a reasonable standard on the stated learning outcomes. There are a number of good reasons for trying to quantify the workload, despite the need for 'typical', 'normally', 'average' and 'reasonable' terms:

1 to achieve fairness – across disciplines and between institutions;
2 to enable greater flexibility – allowing students to include options and electives as part of their studies in order to broaden the curriculum;
3 to permit students to transfer from one institution to another during the course of their studies and gain reasonable recompense for the work done so far;
4 to facilitate stepping-in and stepping-out – allowing students to take breaks and then return to their studies. This is particularly useful for part-time students.

This was resolved by introducing a tariff – a credit – system, by:

■ giving credit ratings to chunks of study;
■ setting a total credit requirement for a particular qualification;
■ equating the unit of measurement – the credit – with a nominal student workload.

At this stage, we urge you to check the system in place in your own institution as there is not a nationally agreed approach; in fact, some HEIs do not use the system at all. To exemplify what we have said so far we will describe a typical model:

■ courses are generally divided into 10-credit, 20-credit and 40-credit chunks, usually called modules;
■ a typical, three-year undergraduate degree comprises 360 credits;
■ the credits are spread evenly over the three levels of the degree – 120 at each level;
■ an undergraduate credit equates to 10 hours of student work (an average student working at a reasonable . . .).

As a result, a typical 10-credit undergraduate unit or module requires 100 nominal hours of student work, including the assessments. Yet only a small part of this will be timetabled – in lectures, laboratories, classes, tutorials, etc. The remainder will be divided between private study and

35

directed study time. Teachers therefore need to take note of this, as they may be responsible for setting directed study work or guiding private study in addition to giving the classes. Directed study could include: setting examples for students to work through; specific reading; direction to watch a particular film/programme/event; providing a reading list that guides but does not constrain students' reading (we note later the value of annotated lists rather than just several pages of references). Some colleagues suggest that there are fixed periods of preparation/ follow-on from classes:

- a couple of hours following-up each lecture, checking and consolidating notes and referring to the primary and secondary literature that was referenced;
- a period of time preparing for a tutorial or seminar, in order that the quality, face-to-face time is used for discussion, elaboration and extension of the basic ideas rather than information giving.

In addition, teachers may need to think about how this directed study is monitored and how feedback is given to students on the work they complete during the time.

In summary, some aspects of the credits sytem may be rather loosely defined, but teachers need to think about how they can direct students to use their time most profitably, and what they can reasonably expect them to do in terms of preparation for classes.

CURRICULUM SHAPE

We have talked of the importance of making links explicit to the students, within the early part of their studies at least. It may be useful to think more broadly about the ways in which the various aspects of the curriculum are related or how the whole curriculum is built. Informing students of the appropriate model of the curriculum could assist them to plan their work and gain a sight of the 'bigger picture'.

Various models are used – a few are illustrated in Figure 2.4. Some modules build one on another, like **Lego** bricks. Other modules are totally free-standing – **satellite**. In other cases all the modules provide component parts, like **jigsaw** pieces, that fit together at the end of the course. During the course, this apparent lack of cohesion needs to be discussed. Sometimes several modules form the basis for a higher level

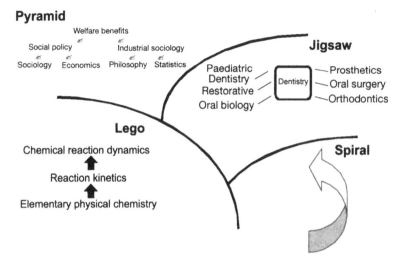

FIGURE 2.4 Curriculum shape

module, like a **pyramid**. And finally in this illustration, the **spiral** curriculum: this is when one returns to a topic at a later stage of the course and topics are revisited periodically in ever more detailed and complex ways. Like the **Lego** structure, the curriculum is additive, and it is essential that students are aware of the progressive nature.

This is not to suggest that the whole curriculum needs to be based on one shape, and you may find that several of the models in Figure 2.4 exist within your course. However, this complexity makes it more important that you understand how your part of the curriculum fits within the broader picture and how all of the curriculum parts fit together, and that you make this clear to students.

QAA CODE OF PRACTICE

We noted in Chapter 1 the transfer of responsibility for the assurance of standards and quality of course provision from an external agency, the QAA, to institutions. However, as you will have noticed from the earlier discussion of FHEQ, level descriptors, Programme Specifications and benchmark statements, this was not done without a raft of control and guidance being put in place. The final aspect of that guidance that we will talk about is the 'Code of Practice for the Assurance of Academic Quality and Standards in Higher Education', usually referred to as the

'Code of Practice'. The code is made up of 10 sections and was released in stages by the QAA, following consultation with HE, between 1998 and 2001. Since 2004 some sections of the code have been revised in the light of experience and changing circumstances, and this is an ongoing process.

The ten sections of the code are:

1   postgraduate research programmes;
2   collaborative provision and flexible and distributed learning (including e-learning);
3   students with disabilities;
4   external examining;
5   academic appeals and student complaints on academic matters;
6   assessment of students;
7   programme approval, monitoring and review;
8   career education, information and guidance;
9   placement learning;
10 recruitment and admissions.

It is the institution's, not the individual's, responsibility to respond to the Code of Practice, and you should find that the processes and procedures in your HEI related to the ten aspects will reflect the precepts and guidance that the code contains.

Five main principles of good practice identified within the code are worthy of mention as they provide useful guides:

1   **Clear definition of responsibilities** – from individuals to committees to departments, both staff and students, should know what is expected of them and what they can expect from each other.
2   **Consistency, fairness and equality** – are applied in all dealings to all involved.
3   **Clear and accessible information** – should be available to all, and it should be up to date.
4   **Competent staff** – you should be able to do the job and receive appropriate training to ensure this.
5   **Monitoring and review** – all processes and procedures should be checked periodically for effectiveness and fairness.

We would not suggest that the code is a great read, but if you are particularly interested in any of the aspects, it is worth taking a look.

VIRTUAL LEARNING ENVIRONMENTS (VLEs)

If you are given responsibility for teaching a course or a number of sessions, it is worth finding out whether the course team make any use of a VLE. If there is a VLE which is already widely used at your institution or in your department, you may find that your students expect you to make materials available for them in this way. Use of the Web and VLEs to make materials available to students 'anytime, anywhere' can assist in study, revision and assignment preparation.

Although VLEs have been available for several years at many HEIs, they are still not universally used. Many factors influence the take-up of new technology among teaching staff and, without rehearsing each of those here, it is worth saying that if you use the campus VLE in your teaching, it may provide you with an opportunity to engage the other teaching staff with new technology too. If you are part of a teaching team working on the same course, using a VLE can ensure that you are able to share resources and be aware of what your students have seen/done in other sessions. This can improve the quality of teaching by ensuring consistency and transparency, and avoiding overlap.

Any discussions about the use of VLEs or other technologies for teaching in a book such as this are necessarily generic because the specific tools at your disposal will depend entirely on what is provided at the institution in which you teach. Training or staff development sessions are usually offered to teaching staff at universities, so it is worth finding out what support is available. If you find yourself in the situation of being the first or only teacher in your team who is making use of technology, it is worth finding out what IT skills or training the students in your department are likely to have had. While some students may expect you to be making use of Web tools and the most up-to-date technology for your teaching, others may be sceptical about its relevance and you should be sensitive to using the VLE to improve the student experience rather than increasing their workload.

 FURTHER RESOURCES

Bologna Process: official website of the Berlin 2003 Conference: www.bologna-berlin2003.de/

Chapter 3

What are your students supposed to learn and be able to do?

LEARNING JOURNEYS – EDUCATIONAL INTENT

'Hi Jenny, fancy coming for a walk?'

'Well, yes, but how far is it? How long will it take? Where are we going? What will we see and do en route? Have I been there before? Is it on the flat or uphill? What clothing and shoes do I need? Is it a walk, a hike or a marathon? Why are we going, wherever it is?'

'Oh, don't worry, you will know when you get there.'

Most of us would not set out on any journey without being clear about the answers to most of Jenny's questions. The same applies to a learning journey: we need to supply a range of information about what is required and we usually do this in the form of aims and learning outcomes. The principal benefit of defining aims and learning outcomes is they provide **guidelines and a common understanding** by course providers (lecturers/teachers) for course takers and 'users' (students and others) **of what is to be achieved** – the nature of the task at hand. Aims and learning outcomes provide students with a guideline of their teachers' expectations and also provide an idea of the standards demanded of them.

Writing aims and learning outcomes is not an exact science. The idea is not to distil the possible outcomes of higher education into a list of competencies or lowest common denominators. The value and outcomes of studying at university cannot, and should not, be prescribed to the last detail. When designing our courses (programmes/modules/ individual sessions) we must have in mind a set of expectations (what students should be able to do as a result of our teaching and their learning) and standards (to what level of competence and expertise). Writing aims and learning outcomes simply makes these expectations and standards more explicit. On a cautionary note, however, beware making claims and demands that cannot be substantiated. For example, a claim that **students will gain a range of transferable skills** may look good on paper, but it needs to be happening 'on the ground' as well. To summarise, aims and learning outcomes provide clarity about the scope of the curriculum and help to focus the learner on what s/he needs to study and achieve.

Unfortunately, there are many terms that are used to describe what Allan (1996) neatly calls **educational intent**: learning outcomes; teaching objectives; competencies; behavioural objectives; goals; aims, among others. This chapter will focus on aims and learning outcomes, but other terms will be defined and discussed as needed for the sake of clarity.

AIMS AND LEARNING OUTCOMES

Distinction

Aims are **broad and general** statements of educational intent, and should inform students of the **overall** purpose of a course, programme or module. They are often written in provider (lecturer/tutor) rather than receiver (student) terms. Learning outcomes, on the other hand, are more focused and indicate what a student will be expected to do at various points during and/or at the end of a course of study. Typically, learning outcomes specify the minimum requirement at the point of assessment for the award of credit; these are the threshold requirements. They may refer to subject-specific concepts, content and skills, or more general (transferable/generic) attributes and abilities. Whatever, they should be written in student rather than in lecturer terms. They are characterised by being:

S pecific	**Provide detail about particular aspects of the expectations.**
M eaningful	**Written in language that is understandable to students and other staff.**
A ppropriate	**Suit the learners' abilities and experience, and satisfy the required standards.**
R ealistic	**Are achievable given time constraints, available resources, etc.**
T estable	**Some measure of progress/achievement towards them can be made.**

There are other interpretations of the SMART acronym, but the particular set here will be used throughout this book.

In essence, then, learning outcomes tell us what a successful student on a course will be able to do on completion of the learning opportunities provided. Some guidance on learning outcomes insists that the statements include the level at which the outcome should be achieved: an indication of **how well** in addition to the 'what?'. This can result in much longer, and more complex, statements that could lead to more confusion over meaning or, worse, less chance of them being read and used by the students. We will, throughout this book, emphasise the need for coherence and congruence – all aspects of the course design process being linked and matched, particularly the essential triangle of learning outcomes, content and assessment. In which case the assessment criteria will give clear guidance on the **how well** and should be read in conjunction with the learning outcomes.

'Will be able to' or 'Should be able to' . . .

Sometimes learning outcomes are written in the form that say that the learner 'will be able to do . . .'. We would advise against this as you have no direct control over what is actually learned. Indeed, you cannot be sure that any learning at all takes place and/or learners may learn additional, unintended, things. As a result, it is far better to say 'will be expected to be able to'. And we are sure that the university's lawyer will be happier with the latter too.

While thinking about being exact with the language that you use, it may be that you are developing or extending what a student should already know or be able to do, in which case it is better to say 'should be better able to . . .'. Outcomes stated in this way take account of existing learning and focus on the notion of progression rather than introduction.

The hierarchy of aims and outcomes

Aims should map into outcomes and vice versa by cascading down or concentrating up – for example, a block of teaching designed to introduce students to historical method, using the life and times of Boudicca as the vehicle (content).

Historical method: a case study of Boudicca

Aim To introduce students to some of the basic problems that concern historians when dealing with sources of evidence.

Outcomes By the end of the module, students should be able (at a basic level) to:
- produce a critical assessment of the sources
- formulate, test and modify a hypothesis
- suggest various explanations for the revolt
- assess the impact and implications of the revolt.

In the above example, note:

- the shift of focus from the tutor (aim) to the student (outcome);
- the statement of level – basic in this case (which in itself needs defining, but still carries meaning);
- that two of the outcomes are not related to the content (Boudicca) at all – the content is simply being used to achieve the generic skill outcome;
- the specificity of the outcomes and the generality of the aim, and the clear mapping between them.

Aims and learning outcomes can be written at a range of levels: university, discipline, programme, module, section and individual session. At each stage they become more specific as one moves from the all-encompassing university claims to the very specific session expectations. For example, the university may claim that all of its graduates will be 'appropriately computer literate'. This is a bit of a meaningless statement as **appropriate** could mean anything from able to plug in a computer to being able to write sophisticated programmes. It does, however, set the marker that shows all curricula in the institution will take heed of the need to consider computer skills. As a result, a particular discipline area may state that all students will have a high proficiency in communication (oral and written) and information technology (IT) skills. Programmes of study within the discipline may be more specific still and expect all students to be able to use word processing and presentation software in order to support their ability to communicate the subject. A module within the programme may aim to develop proficiency in the use of Microsoft Word and PowerPoint. A particular session within the module may focus on certain aspects of Word . . . and so on, becoming ever more specific, and the 'nesting' of the aims and learning outcomes is complete. You will be mostly concerned with the aims and learning outcomes for a module, part of module or individual sessions, but it is important that you are aware of the process of nesting or cascading.

Meaning and significance of other terms

Several terms are used to describe educational intent. We will spend a few paragraphs considering some of the terms that we will not be using, but that you may come across in reading other texts.

Objectives

Aims have a teaching focus, whereas learning outcomes (obviously) are learning focused. But what about objectives? Objectives span both learning and teaching, which can be confusing, and they are sometimes applied to assessment, as detailed in Table 3.1.

In addition, objectives can be interpreted as 'what is intended', whereas outcomes are about 'what has been achieved'. As we are interested in achievement rather than intention and are keen that we are clear about meaning, we will use learning outcomes in preference to objectives.

TABLE 3.1 Objectives

Teaching objectives (**teacher-speak**)	Defined for the teaching process and outlines what the teacher is planning to do, which may not be what the learner is supposed to achieve.
Learning objectives (**student-speak**)	Defined for the learning process and outlines what the learner is meant to achieve.
Assessment objectives (**either-speak**)	Defines what the assessment method is designed to measure: providing an indication of expectations and standards.

Competencies

Learning outcomes can be achieved at a range of levels and, perhaps, in different ways – there is not just one way to get to a destination. While a competency statement is a form of learning outcome, it is much more restricted: typically, it is either achieved or not, passed or failed rather than graded. Behavioural objectives are another restricted form of learning outcomes and describe a result that must be directly observable. Learning outcomes can include behaviours but are much broader – e.g. evaluating. This outcome can be measured in many ways but certainly not only by direct observation.

Writing aims and learning outcomes

Various attempts have been made to describe and categorise what students should be able to do as a result of a period of education, labelled taxonomies. All of these have merit and value, but none seem to apply to all areas and aspects of higher education. Anderson and Krathwohl (2001) include descriptions of 19 such frameworks, in addition to developing a revised and more inclusive version of the Bloom *et al.* (1956) taxonomy. While the Anderson and Krathwohl framework is more carefully constructed and comprehensive, it is too elaborate for the purposes of this text. Instead, we will use a modified and updated version (to represent better the context and expectations of higher education in the twenty-first century) of the original Bloom *et al.* taxonomy. That framework was based on the idea that when thinking about what students should be able to do as a result of their studies in HE, the outcomes can be grouped into three main areas:

1 their intellectual capabilities – what students know and what they can do with what they know
2 their expected attitudes, approaches and values
3 their range of skills – both subject specific and more general/transferable.

Bloom *et al.* described three similar, but slightly more restricted areas that were labelled **domains**, and these were called **cognitive**, **affective** and **psychomotor**.

To help clarify the three areas, an example from Earth Sciences is provided for each (you should be thinking of examples from your own disciplines/areas of learning as you read ours):

Intellectual capabilities – to do with comprehending knowledge and information

45

- Enable students to identify the principal types of igneous rocks and explain how they have formed

Expected attitudes, approaches and values

- Develop the ability to, and responsibility for, critically assessing their own work and that of others

The range of skills

- Use a petrological microscope, to carry out simple optical tests and measurements

(Courtesy of Professor Jane Francis, School of Earth Sciences, University of Leeds)

The examples illustrate that the categories overlap and are interdependent, as one would expect, but this does not reduce the value or the power of the process of defining aims and learning outcomes. The purpose is to give **guidelines and a common understanding of what is to be achieved**, and not to try to prescribe every last detail.

Within each of these three aspects a progression or hierarchy of demand and expectation on the student can be defined. Progression within the attitudinal/approach area may be exemplified by a change in a history student from **realising** the need for a critical approach to the assessment of sources of evidence to habitually **exhibiting** that attitude; or for a medical student **being aware** of what is good practice in terms of bedside manner to **exhibiting** that behaviour as a matter of course. The change here is in the mindset rather than developing understanding or the ability to perform a skill. In terms of skills, this may be seen as a change from the ability to use an instrument or piece of equipment, given a set of detailed instructions, to selection and 'expert' use of equipment in a novel, problem-solving, situation.

WRITING INTELLECTUAL LEARNING OUTCOMES

It is important to consider the progression of intellectual demand on students both within a level and across levels within a programme. Recall, without meaning or realising the significance of information, would be seen as the lowest demand, while the ability to judge, compare and discriminate could be seen as the most demanding. A hierarchy of six levels of intellectual demand is described in Table 3.2, starting at the lowest expectation. Each level on the progression is defined and words that are useful for writing learning outcomes are given: you will note

■ TABLE 3.2 Hierarchy of intellectual demand

Level

1 Knowledge Recalls from prior experience	Ability to recall specific information, to describe known ways of dealing with the information, or to enunciate previously learned general principles or theories

Defines, describes, identifies, lists, matches, names, outlines, recalls, recognises

2 Comprehension Understands, without necessarily relating to other aspects of knowledge	Ability to demonstrate one's understanding by translating or paraphrasing, interpreting information or extrapolating from given data in order to determine likely implications or effects

Classifies, converts, distinguishes between, explains, extends, generalises, paraphrases, predicts, summarises, transforms, translates

3 Application Uses concepts and abstractions in both known and novel situations	Ability to apply abstract principles to particular and concrete situations

Arranges, classifies, computes, demonstrates, employs, extrapolates, modifies, operates, predicts, relates, solves, transfers, uses

4 Analysis Breaking down into components to discover meaning	Clarification of a complex situation by breaking it down into its constituent parts, identifying any relationships between the parts and identifying any organisational structure inherent in the original situation or set of information

Deduces, differentiates, discriminates, distinguishes, estimates, experiments, identifies, infers, orders, separates, subdivides

5 Synthesis Combining elements and aspects into a whole	Bringing together a number of facts or ideas to create a new pattern or structure such as a unique communication, a proposed set of operations or a set of abstract principles which are derived from the original information

Combines, compiles, composes, constructs, creates, designs, formulates, generates, hypothesises, manages, rearranges, relates, revises, summarises

6 Evaluation Judging value and fitness for purpose	Judgements about the value of material or methods for a given purpose

Appraises, assesses, compares, concludes, contrasts, criticises, discriminates, evaluates, judges, justifies, revises, supports

Source: unknown

that they are all verbs, as students are expected to be able **to do** these things.

Some colleagues regard this classification as incomplete, as some of their planned outcomes – creativity, for instance – are not immediately apparent. However, the 'Categories of Transferable Personal Skills' that resulted from the Sheffield Project (1993) included, among others, the following descriptors under the heading of **creative**:

- formulating hypotheses
- extrapolating from the known to the unknown
- working with analogues and parallels
- use of metaphors and analogies
- building on others' ideas.

Many of these descriptors are included or subsumed within the 'definitions' of the higher order skills on the taxonomy that has been described. The first two appear in the **application** and **synthesis** levels. And some colleagues subdivide the application level into 'applying in a known situation' and 'applying in a novel situation'. While the framework is not perfect, it is useful to build on, extend and use rather than dismiss because it is not ideal.

WRITING ATTITUDINAL AND SKILL LEARNING OUTCOMES

If the above provides a useful hierarchy for the intellectual statements, what framework exists for the other – attitudinal and skill – outcomes? A useful progression for thinking about attitudes and approaches is shown in Table 3.3.

TABLE 3.3 Hierarchy of attitudinal demand

Unconscious incompetence	Not knowing what is required/expected
Conscious incompetence	Aware of the need but not the usual behaviour
Conscious competence	Able to demonstrate/enact when thinking about it
Unconscious competence	Demonstrate/enact without thinking – habitual behaviour

TABLE 3.4 Hierarchy of skill demand

Cannot do	Not skilled
Can do, effectively, with instruction	Novice
Can do, effectively, without instruction	Competent
Can write the instructions for doing, or suggest another, equally or more effective, way of doing	Expert

The learning outcomes could be written as transitions from one state to another, for example:

Away from The lecturer has given me all the necessary information and skills.

Towards In professional life, I must study and learn new techniques from a variety of sources.

Other examples of learning outcomes will be given at the end of the chapter.

Similarly, Table 3.4 may provide a valid way to recognise progression in developing a particular skill. Two important course design decisions have to be made. First, how far along each hierarchy do you expect your students to progress at different stages of their course? Perhaps not every student needs to become an expert in every skill, and being able to perform at the stage of novice may suffice at a particular level of the student's studies. Second, what type and sequence of learning opportunities are needed to enable progression from one stage to the next?

OBJECTIONS TO OUTCOMES

Lacks specificity

The problem that the framework is not comprehensive has been mentioned above. Another problem with the Bloom-based classification is that the words can be used at all levels of education. National Curriculum Key Stage 3 requires children in the early years of secondary schooling to **apply** and **analyse**. Similarly, A-level syllabi use the terms. Our view is that we are writing within an HE context, and this automatically implies certain notions of level and prerequisites. The outcomes should link to the assessment criteria and we do not want to become too wordy in our outcomes statements.

49

How, then, would we make clear our expectations at first and second degree level? A balance between being specific without being too limiting or prescriptive is the ideal, but very difficult, target. Specificity can be achieved by writing outcomes that include performance, conditions and criterion aspects, as follows:

Performance   A statement of what the learner should be able to do, which may relate to an intellectual skill, a practical skill or an attitude.

Condition   The conditions under which the performance should occur.

Criterion   The level of performance that is considered acceptable.

For example:

> By level three, students should be able to use secondary as well as primary sources to develop a critical argument, drawing relevant inferences from what they see, hear and read, working either in groups or individually.

Similarly, if you are using technology in your teaching, be specific in your learning outcomes about where and how students will use the technology. If you write learning outcomes for the task, it will help you (and the students) to be clear about what the purpose and result should be.

Outcomes or syllabus

Some colleagues question the difference and value of learning outcomes compared to a list of content headings, because it is the content that they will be covering in their lectures and classes. We have some sympathy with this but, as we would not want to confuse students with both a set of learning outcomes and a content list, we would ask what is the content trying to convey. To illustrate, consider the following example. The Heisenberg Uncertainty Principle could be the content of the lecture, but are the students expected to:

- recall it
- be aware of it
- derive it
- apply it

- describe the life work of Heisenberg
- discuss how uncertain the Uncertainty Principle is?

Answering these questions provides the intended learning outcomes from the lecture on the Heisenberg Uncertainty Principle. Similarly, for the Boudicca example given earlier, the lecture could be about the life and times of that famous queen, but the students need to focus on the comparison of sources and the evidence for the competing historical discourse rather than facts and figures: the learning outcomes should direct the students' attention, and the content (and teaching and learning methods employed) should provide the means by which the students have opportunities to achieve the outcomes.

USING LEARNING OUTCOMES TO GUIDE LEARNING

The preceding pages have, hopefully, convinced you of the value of providing and discussing aims and learning outcomes with your students, and given you ideas on how you can write them. You will probably have the programme and/or module aims and outcomes available to you as a starter, and these will probably be written at the year or semester level – your job will be to provide the specificity at the week or session level. Our approach is to use the ideas for the help they can provide, rather than be limited by them; it is a framework, not a cage. Writing outcomes is a not a precise science, and it is not being suggested that the entire experience, benefit and development achievable from a learning opportunity can be captured by a handful of statements; there is always opportunity for 'unintended learning'. Learning outcomes allow all concerned to share an idea of the journey and landmarks en route, which takes us back to the walk that started this chapter.

Examples of aims and learning outcomes

From a mechanical engineering course – origin unknown

At the end of the course the students' attitudes will have moved:

- **Away from** 'There is a unique solution to this problem.'
- **Towards** 'There are a range of possible solutions to this problem. I must consider all the factors involved, investigate a range of options and recommend the one which I consider to be the most suitable.'

51

- **Away from** 'The lecturer has given me all the necessary information and skills.'
- **Towards** 'In professional life, I must study and learn new techniques from a variety of sources.'

At the end of the course the students will be able to communicate their findings accurately and completely in either oral or written form to 'clients' who are assumed to have a rudimentary technical background but who are not experts in the subject. The presentation should be as brief as possible, consistent with the 'clients' gaining the information and understanding necessary for them to act on the findings and to justify them to their superiors.

From Tomorrow's Doctors, General Medical Council, December 1993

At the end of the course of undergraduate medical education the student will have acquired and will demonstrate attitudes essential to the practice of medicine, including:

a) respect for patients and colleagues that encompasses, without prejudice, diversity of background and opportunity, language, culture and way of life;

b) the recognition of patients' rights in all respects, and particularly in regard to confidentiality and informed consent;

c) approaches to learning that are based on curiosity and the exploration of knowledge rather than on its passive acquisition, and that will be retained throughout professional life;

d) ability to cope with uncertainty.

Example from mathematics

This is an interesting use of the verb, object and context approach to provide very clear outcomes. In the version that the students received the terms were removed. They are also labelled as knowledge (K) or skill (S) outcomes.

On completion of the module, students will be better able to:

- choose, compare and contrast (verbs) simple methods for exploring data (object) on a single variable, or the relationship between two variables (context) (K);

- calculate (verb) statistical power and required sample size (object) for situations that can be analysed using one or two sample t-tests (context) (K);
- write (verb) coherently structured and referenced statistical reports (object) using information from more than one source (context) (S);
- effectively manage (verb) time (object) when working to a deadline (context) (S);
- plan, design and carry out (verbs) simple statistical analyses (object) on an open ended problem (context) (S);
- use (verb) the statistics package (object) to carry out standard tests and calculations (context) (S);
- work together (verb) to present results in oral and written form (object) as part of a group (context) (S).

(Courtesy of Dr Paul Baxter, University of Leeds)

By making specific reference to the use of technology in the learning outcome, students will have no confusion as to what to use the technology for:

- Working individually and posting into the online discussion room, students should be able to identify in writing six potential advantages of using . . . on the . . . and reference three current writers on this topic (knowledge).
- Using the online discussion room students will gather and share relevant data relating to . . . and analyse and create a summary of . . . within the room (comprehension).
- Students will work as a group to analyse a given online journal article identifying potential problem areas or weaknesses in the research methodology offered. Individual students will post (in the course discussion area) questions they would ask the researcher (analysis).
- Students should be able to individually compile a list . . . and then work as a group online to assemble, collate, agree and prioritise a final list . . . (synthesis).
- Using the online discussion room, students will work as a team to record their project working and processes and then orally present their findings to their tutorial group making reference to those online records (application).
- Students will use the online discussion room to debate, question and judge received opinion on topics of . . . (evaluation).

53

Aims of the Department of Modern Deep Space Studies

The course will provide students with:

- a high proficiency in passive and active skills in Klingon and other selected Deep Space languages;
- a broad and balanced understanding of the literature, culture, history and society of the Klingons, other selected Deep Space peoples and subject peoples of the Klingon empire;
- a high proficiency in communication (oral and written), analysis, comment and argument, in the areas outlined above, and IT skills;
- on the ground experience of life in the Klingon empire and other selected Deep Space territories.

(Originals courtesy of Dr David Collins
(University of Leeds), adapted by Chris Butcher)

 FURTHER RESOURCES

A wide range of guides and ideas (and see also the Resources and publications section) on the Oxford Centre for Staff and Learning Development website at: www.brookes.ac.uk/services/ocsd/2_learntch/2_learnt.html

Tomorrow's Professor Mailing List: a hundred postings to your mailbox each year that cover a range of Learning and Teaching (L&T) issues, and includes articles, summaries of books and ideas for development. The list is sponsored by the Stanford University Center for Teaching and Learning (http://ctl.stanford.edu). An archive of all past postings can be found at: http://ctl.stanford.edu/Tom prof/index.shtml

 FURTHER READING

Hussey, T. and Smith, P., 2003. The Uses of Learning Outcomes. *Teaching in Higher Education*, Vol. 8, No. 3, pp. 357–368. This paper argues that learning outcomes need to be reclaimed from their current use as devices for monitoring and audit, and returned to their proper use in aiding good teaching and learning.

Chapter 4

Matching your content to outcomes and not the other way around

CONTEXT

For many new teachers, it is the case that you are told exactly what to teach and you have little, if any, freedom to select the content: you have a set seminar series that cover topics x, y and z; the laboratory sessions will include the following experiments/topics. In such cases, this chapter will have, at this stage, less value to you as we are taking as our starting point that you are free to select the content.

Alternatively, you may be bound by the course Programme Specification, and the learning outcomes are prescribed, but you have the opportunity to select the most appropriate content to enable the students to successfully achieve the outcomes. Then again, you may be designing a new module or updating existing modules. In these cases, the ideas presented in this chapter will help you when you are considering the content that you should select.

What do I know that I can tell them?

Most of us, when asked to teach a topic, start by thinking about the content. Questions such as 'What do I know that I can tell them?' or 'Who are the best authors or references for this subject?' dominate our thinking. This is only natural because we, as academics, trade in understanding, insights, thinking, analysis, synthesis and creativity, but our currency is knowledge, information, facts, data.

When it comes to deciding the appropriate content for our teaching sessions it must be the learning outcomes that guide us to decide the content that we will use. If the learning outcome is a knowledge statement, the choices are restricted: principles, laws and bibliographical details cannot be changed. But you can select the range of examples and applications that illustrate the principles and demonstrate the significance of the laws, and choose the life episodes that illustrate the significance of the person and their work. There may be, of course, several choices of content that could be used in order to enable students to learn a particular concept, ability or skill, and then it becomes a matter of personal choice or selection based on the available resources. This situation is well illustrated by considering the common higher education learning outcome that students are able to **evaluate**: the selection of content in a chemistry course would be significantly different from that chosen, say, in an English literature class, but the planned outcome is the same in both instances.

Harden (1986/1998) suggested four useful guides to selecting content. These can be useful as, while they constrain us to select on the basis of the learning outcomes, they allow free reign over the breadth and depth of the content of the discipline. In the original work, Harden's four categories – mainstream, precursor, opportunistic and supportive – were defined. Our interpretation is a little different in order that the categories are applicable to all disciplines and curricula, whereas Harden was thinking particularly of the medical curriculum.

Mainstream It directly contributes to one or more of the planned learning outcomes or course aims. As noted above, there may be many different examples of content that could be selected within the subject area – one of several different novels, case studies, industrial applications, or geographic regions. Selection may be on familiarity, enjoyment, resource availability or a topic of one aspect of your research. Or it may be influenced by one of the remaining three categories.

Precursor It is core knowledge or a skill that is needed for a later part of the course – in order to do x, you need to know/understand/be able to do y. Selecting content of this type only begins when you start to distil the learning outcomes into some sort of logical stages and sequence, and decide how they can be achieved.

Opportunistic This content provides both core and added-value opportunities to learn. A particular demonstration or experiment may be included as it illustrates specific, essential ideas or facts. In addition, the analysis of the data from the event may provide opportunities to develop additional intellectual skills: analytical, computational, ability to formulate, hypothesise. Alternatively, the works of two authors may be presented as they provide core details about the work of the authors, the period and context in which they lived, the significance of their contribution and the meaning of their writing. In addition, comparison of the two may give insight into a range of other ideas and principles, and give opportunities to develop and practise vital analytical, comparative and critical thinking skills. The bonus here is that the same content can provide for the differing abilities of the students that you are teaching. Some may only grasp the core ideas, while others are able to go much further. As discussed in Chapter 7, your students will have a wide variety of learning needs and preferences. Also, they will have a mix of previous experience, knowledge, understanding and ability, and the challenge is to provide for all.

Supportive As the word suggests, this is content that illustrates and illuminates other aspects of the course – an industrial, commercial or real-life example, for instance. The significance is not in the detail of the case study or example, and we have to beware here that students are clear about the value and do not see it as more 'facts to learn', but in the clarification, elaboration and richness that it brings to other concepts and content.

Harden's four guides, described above, are a useful start to the topic of selecting content. We will return to other methods later in the chapter, but first let us consider the next question that often comes to mind when we are asked to teach a topic.

How much?

If we start by thinking about 'what?', then almost certainly the next question is 'how much?'. Before we begin to think about an answer, the question needs to be put into context.

Most UK universities use a credit framework for their taught courses, with many using 360 credits for a first, undergraduate degree and 180 credits for a taught, postgraduate, Master's degree. Each credit equates to a fixed number of student hours of work or a 'nominal' workload. In our institution, each credit represents the outcome of 10 hours of student work. It is essential that you check out the system in your institution as it may differ in some of the details; we will be using the approach in our university to illustrate ideas here.

Typically, then, a three-year undergraduate course comprises 360 credits, 120 being taken in each of the years. The 120 credits are taken as a series of 10- and 20-credit modules or units, and occasionally, and typically in the final year, as 30- or 40-credit dissertation or project modules. Therefore, a student could be taking between 6 and 12 modules or units in a year, probably equally split across the two semesters that comprise the academic year in most institutions now. Let us take a 10-credit module as an example, as this would represent 100 hours of student work. This time would include all the timetabled teaching, self-directed and private study work, preparation for assessment and the assessment itself. In this period, a student should be able to successfully achieve the learning outcomes that are set for the module. Some credit schemes are more clear about the standard of achievement expected within the time frame than others. Again, you need to check in your context whether the expected standard is pass, average mark or some other standard.

In addition to having different credit schemes in different universities (and some do not use a credit scheme at all) you will find that there are different norms for timetabled teaching (sometimes labelled 'contact time') in different disciplines. It is not unusual to have 30 hours of contact in an engineering module, while there may be only a few hours in an arts subject. However, it is important to remember that the total time – contact time, self-directed and private study work, preparation for assessment and the assessment itself – should be the same whatever the discipline for equal credit-rated modules.

You may feel that much of this detail is not important to you, but we assure you it is needed (precursor content). Returning to the question of 'how much?', in order to make this decision you need to find out the total hours that your topic should take – taught, directed work, private study and assessment – in order to plan appropriately what you will be able to include in the face-to-face teaching time and what you will need to set in terms of directed reading/activities in the students' private study time. The combination of these two aspects of their work is the total time that they should be taking, on average, to achieve the planned learning outcomes.

Armed with this knowledge, you can think realistically about the balance between contact and directed time, which aspects of the content best fit where and what the sequence should be in order that taught classes support private study and preparation time best suits and gives useful precursor thinking and learning to taught sessions.

A rather simplistic, but useful way to think about this is another four-category model that is illustrated in Figure 4.1.

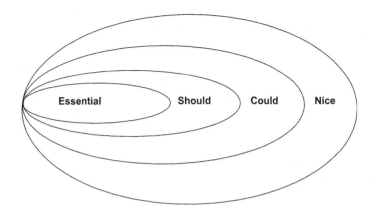

FIGURE 4.1 Enough is enough

Essential The basics (knowledge and understanding), which permit further study and development of the topic. Perhaps this is the material that must be covered in the taught sessions. Also, this might be seen as the absolute minimum that would enable a student to achieve the threshold requirement of the learning outcomes. It would certainly include all the most difficult concepts and ideas within the topic that the students must study.

Should Develops the **essential** into a broader and deeper grasp of the topic. This might be through directed reading and associated tasks (which may include feedback on achievement by you). **Essential** and **should** together probably represent sufficient for an average student to achieve, in the nominal hours, a reasonable standard in the assessment.

Could A further deepening and broadening of the topic, extending detail, examples, application and insights.

Nice All there is to know, and some more besides.

Thinking about the categories of **essential, should, could** and **nice** can be a useful way of ensuring a balance within the workload of a module and may also suggest teaching/study methods. **Essential** material might need to be delivered through taught classes in order to ensure coverage and explanation, while **could** material may be part of directed, extension study based on an annotated reading list (as discussed in Chapter 7). Alternatively, if the course is mainly delivered through private study with very little group contact time, the essential aspects may be the ones that you consider are the hardest for the students to deal with on their own, and so should be the focus of the class contact periods in order that you are able to monitor progress.

We should state at this stage that we are not expecting you to balance the **mainstream** with the **essential**, the **precursor** with the **could** – these are two different ways of looking at the same task and one approach might appeal more than the other. Designing teaching and learning opportunities will reflect your preferences as the teacher, but do remember to think about the range of styles and preferences of the students, and the limitations of the resources available. All we are aiming to do is to provide you with a range of tools to help you think through the task.

There are other matrices, maps and grids that will enable you to determine and select the content that should comprise modules. While all may be used for designing teaching, it may be worth considering whether the students would gain from sharing the information also – particularly the concept/content map and the schedule – as a means of supporting learning.

MATRICES, MAPS AND GRIDS

Concept/content maps

These charts show the relationship(s) between concepts, ideas and content, and allow mapping of the content territory. This idea is useful as a means of selecting lecture content and it can be used to develop a map for a section of a course, a module or a complete programme. Some colleagues term these 'mind maps', but they are not true mind maps as Buzan (2000) describes them.

Talking through the example shown in Figure 4.2 will illustrate best the idea. Start with the main topic heading in the centre – in this instance **presentations** – and around that list the major subtopics that need to be considered if a comprehensive coverage of the subject matter is being provided. For each of these subtopics the group of aspects that make up the theme are built up. Following a particular branch, if **confidence** is an important aspect of presentation skills, then **body language**, **eye contact** and **dress** are all themes that would need to be covered. Going a stage further would show the subthemes around **body language** – **stance**, **gestures**, **open/closed**, etc.

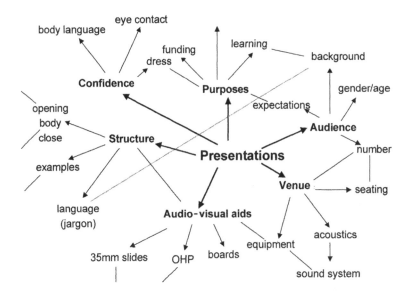

FIGURE 4.2 Content map

The aim is to give representative titles rather than elaborate descriptions. Notice that the topic, subtopics, aspects and subaspects are joined by arrows to show the connections. The notion is that these should be clearly presented and well-structured maps, but this is not always possible to achieve even with redrawing. Some links between topics may have to be drawn across or around the periphery of the map (one instance – background to jargon – is shown). However, these are not pieces of artwork – they are organic, changing as necessary, maps of the content terrain.

The map could be used to think through which content will be selected to deliver the planned learning outcomes, or to consider the **essential, should,** etc., or the **mainstream, precursor,** etc. Maps such as this could be provided to students, if appropriately introduced and discussed, to show them the links between the various components of a module or unit, providing an holistic view. In addition, they could be used to show links to other parts of the taught curriculum: 'actually, audio-visual aids is dealt with in the media module and so will not be considered here, but you will need to transfer the ideas and apply them to the work that we will be doing in this module . . . .'.

TABLE 4.1 Linking methods to outcomes

Topic				
	Subtopic			
		Aspect		
		Aspect		
		Aspect		
			Subaspect	
			Subaspect	
		Aspect		
	Subtopic			
		Aspect		
		Aspect		

If you are not keen on a map as a way of visualising or representing this information, a hierarchical content list could be used, as shown in Table 4.1. As in a book with chapter headings and subheadings, this gives a neat and logical structure, but if the aim is to show how it all relates, this model is less effective.

Schedules

Construction of a schedule provides an opportunity to check workloads, deadline clashes, timetable arrangements, room and staff requirements, and appropriateness of teaching sessions, and to ensure that students (and staff) are clear about the arrangements for a module. In Table 4.2, the content has been related to a 'set text' also, to enable appropriate forward reading. In addition to the timeline of information, another valuable outcome of the exercise is the avoidance of clustering of deadlines. The schedule that is given below covers a complete, semester-long, thirteen-week, module. But the same idea could be applied to a few weeks of teaching or a section of a module; the purpose is to lay out all the details in an easily accessible manner.

Outcomes–content matrix

If schedules and concept maps are helpful ways of organising and selecting content, then this matrix provides a useful means of ensuring

▓ TABLE 4.2 Teaching schedule

Week beginning (week no.)	Chapter title (chapter no.) (Cohen and Manion, 1989)	Assessment	Lectures (Tues. and Weds., 10–11)	Tutorials (Thurs., 10–12)
2005 – 2006				
3 Oct. (2)	The Nature of Enquiry (1)		T & W	
10 Oct. (3)	Historical Research (2)		T & W	
17 Oct. (4)	Surveys (4)			Th
24 Oct. (5)	Case Studies (5)			Th
31 Oct. (6)	Correlation Research (6)	Assignment 1	T & W	
7 Nov. (7)	Action Research (9)		T & W	
14 Nov. (8)	Triangulation (11)			Th
21 Nov. (9)	The Interview (14)	Assignment 1 returned		Th
28 Nov. (10)	Personal Constructs	Assignment 2	T & W	
5 Dec. (11)	*Revision week*	Assignment 2 can be collected	T & W	Th (optional)
10 Jan. (17)	*Examination weeks*			
Dates of events	Content (may relate to set text(s)	Deadlines: submit and return	Teaching sessions	

that the chosen content relates to the learning outcomes and shows that coverage is complete without undue repetition. It comprises a simple two-dimensional grid that lists the outcomes on one axis and the content on the other. For brevity in the example, Table 4.3, letters have been used to represent the outcomes (a to f) and content (G to M). Then it is just a case of thinking about which outcomes are enabled by content G and ticking boxes to show this, and then moving onto content H and so on, Table 4.4. Alternatively, you could work from the outcomes and tick the content boxes – either way around works.

From the matrix in Table 4.4 it becomes apparent:

- some content does not relate to any outcomes (L);
- an outcome is not covered by the selected content (e);

TABLE 4.3 Outcomes–content matrix

				Subject content			
		G	H	I	J	K	L	M

Educational outcomes	G	H	I	J	K	L	M
a							
b							
c							
d							
e							
f							

TABLE 4.4 Completed outcomes–content matrix

Subject content

Educational outcomes	G	H	I	J	K	L	M
a	✓	✓	✓				
b		✓			✓		
c			✓		✓		✓
d	✓		✓				
e							
f				✓			✓

- possible repetition – it might be worth looking at G and I as they overlap considerably;
- possible redundancy – is J needed?

(It may be decided that the repetition provided by G and I is a useful revision, and so is best left, whereas J is not needed, so is best deleted. This would make room for new content N that addresses outcome e.)

Obviously, this is rather a crude tool, but the process of completion, rather than the final grid, is the important part as the process ensures that we think carefully about the links and that we solve any inconsistencies that arise.

Before leaving grids, it is worth considering another two: the **skills development matrix** and the **progression of practical skills matrix**. Both of these are for reviewing level and/or programme detail rather than for an individual module. Their purpose is to check how individual modules contribute to the 'big picture', thus ensuring coherence and avoiding unnecessary repetition. Thinking this through for your programme will give you the big picture and help you to see where your teaching fits in the overall scheme. Both matrices will inform you of the attributes and skills that you can assume and which you need to contribute to.

Skills development matrix

This matrix analyses when skills (both key/generic and subject-specific) are introduced (I) to the students (if appropriate), then practised (P) by the students and, again if appropriate, assessed (A). The values of this analysis are self-evident:

- progression of skills – staff can assume (or not) degrees of competence
- comprehensive coverage – all the necessary skills are incorporated into the curriculum
- avoidance of undue repetition.

For an existing programme, the first stage in developing this matrix would be agreement by teaching staff as to which skills need to be included: this would need to be informed by the subject benchmark statement. Some form of audit would follow this stage in order to find

TABLE 4.5 Skills matrix

BSc Human Biology				
Level 1 Skills				
Skill	HUMB1020	HUMB1030	HUMB1050	HUMB1060
Discipline-specific skills				
Microscopy		I P A		
Tissue culture				
Photomicrography				
Dissection				
Interpretation of medical images	I P A			
Use of specialised equipment				
Correct use of anatomical terminology	I P A	I P A		
Transferable skills				
Time management	P	P	P	P
Independent learning	P	P	P	P
Co-operative learning	I		P	P
Library skills	P			
Written communication		I P A	P A	P
Oral communication			P	P
Information technology		P		
Data analysis and interpretation				
Group working				
Critical evaluation of literature				
Project design and implementation				
Self-evaluation				
	Introduced	Practised	Assessed	

Source: Reproduced with kind permission of the Centre for Human Biology, University of Leeds.

out what is already happening. The teaching team would then need to review the outcomes of the audit and make appropriate, agreed changes. The result would be a coherent strategy for skills development. The example, Table 4.5, is part of the level one grid for a Human Biology course. The left-hand column shows the agreed list of skills (separated as discipline-specific and transferable), and the top line shows four of the compulsory modules. The grid has then been completed – audited – to show what was happening; you will note some of the anomalies that the audit had shown. The group went on to design a coherent grid for level one and then looked at progression into levels two and three.

Skill maps have become an integral part of Programme Specifications that are required for HE courses, based on QAA guidelines, and the skills are those that are listed in the benchmarking statements. So this information should exist for your course and, therefore, will be worth finding.

Progression of practical skills matrix

The final matrix detailed here is useful for reviewing the development of practical skills and the ability to tackle student-centred project work. This idea, illustrated in Table 4.6, could be applied to a range of expectations – skills, attitudes and attributes – but the example in this instance is restricted to the development of competency in practical/laboratory work.

The labels in the first column, labelled stage, are not really important. It is the 'freedom' that the student has over deciding the aim of the work, selection of materials and choice of method and the degree of uncertainty/novelty of the answers and outcomes that is key. Ideally, students would follow a regime that moves them from carefully structured and guided work (exercises and structured enquiries) to a position of greater freedom as they gain confidence and ability. A jump from **exercise** to **open-ended enquiries** could leave students unsure and ill-prepared, and will probably result in failure or a reduction in the effectiveness of the learning experience.

This grid provides best value when it is customised in the first instance; this means that the labels in the first column are changed to match those used in the department, and the open/closed tags are changed to suit the conventions of the department. This customisation may also require that rows are added to or deleted from the grid in order to ensure that it fully represents the situation in the department. The next stage is to check that the existing situation provides a coherent and progressive

67

TABLE 4.6 Practical skills matrix

Aspect ⇒ Stage ⇓	Aim	Materials	Method	Answer
Demonstration	given	given	given	given
Exercise	given	given	given	open
Structured enquiry	given	given – part or whole	open or part given	open
Open-ended enquiry	given	open	open	open
Project	open	open	open	open

pathway for the students, and if it does not, to decide what needs adding, changing or deleting. The same sort of grid could be envisaged for developing dissertation skills – starting with a structured essay, then allowing negotiation of titles, moving on to free-choice of essay titles, then mini-project, and/or mini dissertation, and finally the full dissertation in the final year.

These two examples of skills grids should remind you that a vital part of any content selection is knowing where your students are starting from – what you are able to build on – and a brief discussion of that concludes this chapter.

What do they already know? What can I assume?

The skills grids show you quickly what can be assumed. Reading the learning outcomes of earlier and concurrent modules should give you another guide. Similarly, the level statements provide an indication of the sorts of attributes and ability that can be built on. Talking to colleagues and asking students enables a fuller picture to be drawn. Some repetition, particularly of difficult concepts, is valuable for revision and reinforcement. However, too much overlap can demotivate students: progression and challenge are essential aspects of the design process.

FURTHER RESOURCES

Subject Networks

The Higher Education Academy in the UK includes the Subject Network, with the role of developing and transferring good teaching and learning practices in subject disciplines. There are 24 Subject Centres in the network and they provide a range of resources, events and interest groups. It will be worth your while to check out what is available (see www.heacademy.ac.uk/Subject Network.htm). An important part of the Subject Network activities is the SNAS database, designed for staff new to teaching in HE (see www.heacademy. ac.uk/snasdatabase.asp).

Chapter 5

Horses for courses
Selecting the appropriate teaching and learning methods

INTRODUCTION

The continuing theme in this chapter is one of coherence: the curriculum comprises a number of parts and aspects, but they must all fit together to produce a cohesive and coherent whole. Some suggest that it is important that students do not see the gaps, that it should be a seamless curriculum. However, students experience the taught curriculum in bits: they go to lectures, laboratory classes, seminars/tutorials, use the VLE, etc. It is important to tell students how all of the parts fit together and what they should do to glue the parts in place.

This is particularly important for students in the first year of their degree. The counter argument is that they are being *spoon-fed* and that they must learn to be autonomous, to become independent learners. We agree that students must learn to become independent learners, but would emphasize the words **learn to**. While one way of learning to swim is to jump into the deep end of the pool without a float or water wings, we believe that there are more efficient ways.

The following situation that we encountered illustrates, with unfortunate consequences, the need to communicate expectations. A group of first-year students thought the detailed and comprehensive lecture notes that they were provided with gave all that was required in terms of content. Indeed, the notes were very informative and provided very detailed explanations, and invariably they had numerous references attached. The teaching staff perceived the handouts as the skeleton, and that the references (and the reading lists in the module handbooks) provided the means to add the flesh on the bones. This was not picked up by the students until it was too late, and the examinations came around.

The messages of this chapter are: coherence (reminding you about Biggs' notion of constructive alignment – see p. 26); developing autonomy (students should be independent learners by the time they reach level three at the latest); and progression. Selecting the appropriate methods for teaching and learning to enable these to come about requires you to consider options carefully, taking account of resources and time, and then communicating your expectations to students.

WHAT CAN YOU DO?

You may not have the freedom to select the type of teaching/learning approach you use: you may be given responsibility for a set of tutorials, series of computer classes or block of laboratory classes. But you may well be deciding and planning individual classes. We will discuss the sorts of methods and activities that you may include in the classes later in the chapter, but first, it is worth spending a short time thinking about the various methods of teaching and learning that are available to us and deciding what students can best achieve. However, there is a vital stage before that. We need to look at how students learn: what are the important conditions that promote learning and, just as important, what do we know that hinders learning?

Helping students learn

You may be aware that there has been considerable debate in the last few years about the efficacy and significance of some of the models of learning, and associated ideas about learning styles and learning preferences, which have been promulgated over that last twenty years or so. Despite this uncertainty, there are a number of facts about learning that we are clear about. The first is that there are no guarantees: we cannot guarantee that a particular learning opportunity – be it a lecture, a seminar, computer-based learning or other method – will result in the same degree of learning, any learning even, for the group of students who experience it. Neither can we be sure that a particular approach is the best for all students – they have individual preferences, styles and motivations. We do know that the following factors can help students to learn (but learning can occur even if these are not present):

1   **Building on foundations** – new ideas and knowledge are linked to existing frameworks.
2   **Guidance on what is to be learned** – clear learning outcomes are linked to detailed assessment criteria and grade descriptors.

71

3   **Processing activities** – opportunities to discuss and rehearse ideas and concepts as they are met.

4   **Application activities** – opportunities to use ideas, and to extend and enhance understanding by being challenged.

5   **Structure** – an organized and sequenced pathway through concepts.

6   **Feedback on learning** – timely information on how successful, or not, learning has been.

7   **Resources necessary for the task** – paper and electronic, and appropriate access to tutors.

8   **Support structure** – help to deal with both academic and pastoral issues as they arise.

When planning for successful teaching and student learning, these eight factors should be borne in mind. A ninth, motivation, is very important also. Students wanting or needing to learn – intrinsic and extrinsic motivation – is a vital ingredient.

These factors are founded on a range of ideas concerning student learning: surface and deep learning, the Kolb learning cycle (Kolb, 1984) and Race's 'ripples on a pond model' (Race, 2005) in particular. You should refer to the Brown (2004) materials that accompany this series (see www.routledgefalmer.com/series/KGETHE/).

With these thoughts in mind, we will consider the range of teaching methods that is available. 'We have always done it that way' (and the implication therefore that it both works and is the best way) and cost (time and resources) are often barriers to rethinking teaching approaches. The choice of method must, of course, take account of resources – staff, space and equipment. But it is worth stepping back on occasion and asking whether the usual and traditional are still the ideal. This is not to suggest, however, that innovation is synonymous with the best.

WHAT CAN THE VARIOUS TEACHING AND LEARNING METHODS BEST ACHIEVE?

Factors that can direct choice of teaching and learning method include:

- student grouping (large or small group, individual, distance or face-to-face);
- role of the tutor (tutor-led or tutor-less; directing, guiding or monitoring);

- educational technology (supported or mediated by);
- minds-on (theory based) or hands-on (practically based);
- stage in the programme (to ensure progression).

The methods that we use need to reflect the needs of the students, the type of content that is being used to satisfy particular learning outcomes and the resources available. To select appropriate methods, we need to be clear about what we are trying to achieve and have a detailed knowledge of what the various methods can offer.

Linking methods to outcomes

The various teaching methods available provide a wealth of opportunities to develop particular attributes and abilities. Table 5.1 (there have been various, similar examples in the literature) attempts to highlight the particular strengths as we see them of some common teaching approaches. (Reminders of some terms are given below the table.) The purpose of the table is to direct your thinking towards selection of the method to achieve defined outcomes rather than provide debate about the exact location of the ticks. (This will depend on definition of the terms, which in turn reflect context and practice. Starting with a blank table and adding your own ticks is another useful way of thinking about what the various methods mean to you and can offer your students. In addition, you may want to add to the 'focus of learning' columns in order to suit your particular discipline.) Alternatively, you may care to use the table to carry out an audit of the methods you use and the reason(s) the various approaches are selected in a module that you teach. Another value of this table is that it promotes ideas about diversifying techniques in order to add coverage of attributes and interest.

Linking methods to student factors

Again, we do not wish to debate our placing of the ticks, crosses and question marks, but to promote thinking about various methods from the (ideal?) student perspective. Table 5.2 builds on an original idea by Kuethe (1968). As before, you could start from a blank table and consider your views. And you might like to consider whether it would be worth asking students what they think. Whatever your approach, the important point is that you consider methods on their particular strengths and merits.

73

TABLE 5.1 Linking methods to outcome

Method	Focus of the learning								
	Intellectual capabilities		Attitudes, approaches and values		Skills		Group skills	Ability to communicate
	K C A*	A S E**	Aware	Habit	Guidance	Expert	Develop	Develop
Lecture	✓		✓					
Tutorial		✓	✓	✓	✓	✓	✓	✓
Seminar	✓	✓	✓	✓				✓
Demonstration	✓		✓					
Laboratory		✓	✓	✓	✓	✓	✓	
Workshop		✓	✓	✓	✓	✓	✓	✓
Role play		✓	✓	✓			✓	✓
Simulations		✓		✓		✓	✓	
Resource-based learning	✓	✓	✓		✓			
Projects		✓		✓		✓	✓	✓

*K C A: Knowledge, Comprehension and Application (considered as low order).
**A S E: Analysis, Synthesis and Evaluation (considered as high order).

TABLE 5.2 Linking methods to student outcomes

Attribute ⇒ Method ⇓	Directs attention	Promotes motivation	Maintains interest	Provides immediate feedback	Allows student to progress at own rate
Lecture	✓	✓/?	✓/?	✗	✗
Tutorial	✓	✓	✓	✓	✓
Seminar	✓	✓/?	?	✓	✓/?
Demonstration	✓	✓/?	✓	✗	✗
Laboratory	✓	✓/?	✓	✓	✓
Workshop	✓	✓	✓	✓	✓
Role play	✓	✓	✓	✓	✓
Simulations	✓	✓	✓	✓	✓
Resource-based learning	✓	✓	✓	✗	✓
Projects	✓	✓	✓	✗	✓

Linking outcomes to methods

Another approach, shown in Table 5.3, is to start from the outcomes, and this table is based on an idea from the Oxford Centre (1990). The Bloom taxonomy is used to provide the learning outcomes hierarchy, and for each particular demand a range of methods based on appropriateness, practicality and availability of resources has been proposed.

Don't restrict your thinking to common methods

Bourner and Flowers (1998) provided an interesting set of six purposes of higher education, on which they elaborate in their paper:

- disseminate knowledge;
- develop the capability to use ideas and information;
- develop the ability to test ideas and evidence;
- develop the ability to generate ideas and evidence;
- personal development;
- develop the capacity to plan and manage one's own learning.

TABLE 5.3 Linking outcomes to methods

Outcomes	Teaching method or student activity
1 Intellectual capabilities – what students know and what they can do with what they know	
The students should be better able to:	
Recall from prior experience	lectures; reading; practical work; glossaries; online materials
Use concepts and abstractions in both known and novel situations	worked examples; case studies; practical work; placements; industrial/commercial visits; projects; dissertations
Judge value and fitness for purpose	review and compare articles; case studies; role play
2 Range of skills – both subject specific and more general/transferable	
The students should demonstrate the ability to:	
Communicate in a range of ways	essays; reports; dissertations; postings in a VLE; presentations; tutorial and seminar work
Research, select and organise information	using the library (databases and catalogues); web searches; essay plans
Work in teams	group work; group projects; online debates
3 Expected attitudes, approaches and values	
The students should increasingly demonstrate:	
Autonomous learning	reading around subject; reviewing and reflecting on abilities in learning journals or progress files; use of discussion rooms in VLEs
Concern for accuracy	self-assessment tasks; peer marking; responding to feedback
Ethical approach	case studies; role play; placements

In addition, they suggested a wide range of teaching approaches, some quite novel, which can be used both to support and challenge the norm. They include assessment techniques as teaching methods – a realistic, if unusual, perspective.

In your thinking about methods you should consider how online communication tools such as asynchronous discussion rooms and web-logs provide new spaces for group work. Once it would have been necessary to have all your students together in one room at the same time for a debate or role play, but now it is possible to conduct a similar activity online with the added advantages of anonymity or working via avatars if desired.

In Chapter 2 the Seven Principles for Good Practice in Undergraduate Education were listed, (Gamson and Chickering, 1987). These were updated to include the use of technology (Chickering and Ehrmann, 1996). The later version describes the way that contact between students and staff can be extended and enhanced, time 'on task' can be focused and feedback can be given.

Traditionally, time-delayed communication took place in education through the exchange of homework, either in class or by mail (for more distant learners). Such time-delayed exchange was often a rather impoverished form of conversation, typically limited to three con-versational turns:

1 The instructor poses a question (a task).
2 The student responds (with homework).
3 The instructor responds some time later with comments and a grade.

The conversation often ends there; by the time the grade or comment is received, the course and student are off on new topics.

Now, however, electronic mail, computer conferencing, and the World Wide Web increase opportunities for students and faculty to converse and exchange work much more speedily than before, and more thoughtfully and 'safely' than when confronting each other in a classroom or faculty office. Total communication increases and, for many students, the result seems more intimate, protected, and convenient than the more intimidating demands of face-to-face communication with faculty.

(Chickering and Ehrmann, 1996, p. 4)

77

ONLINE SEMINARS

Planning for outcomes

Successful achievement of learning outcomes in online discussion groups requires forward planning on your part; think carefully about what you want to achieve and how this will link to the learning outcomes of the class you have planned. You might consider:

- enabling students to present course materials outside of the classroom. This can free up valuable class time to use for discussions, activities and collaborative work;
- supporting student group projects by archiving discussions, collating material or recording planning notes when it is difficult to find time to meet;
- encouraging academic discussion and written argument or extending discussion beyond the limits of class times;
- structuring discussion through specific question-and-answer tasks or online debates;
- sharing student experience and peer support.

Online discussion provides a different environment for learning. It should not be seen as **replicating** face-to-face discussion, and applying traditional assumptions about classrooms to online discussions may limit our understanding and realisation of the full potential of this new medium (Harasim, 1989, p. 50). In most cases of teaching on campus, online communication should not be seen as **replacing** face-to-face discussion either. Online tasks should link to face-to-face teaching, **enhancing** it by providing flexibility of working. Activities can be started online as preparation and extended in class, or begun in class and extended online.

Changing the classroom dynamic

As well as making content available outside traditional classroom structures, the nature of online communication allows students to participate on an equal footing. Students who seem reluctant to participate in classroom discussion may flourish online and vice versa (McSporran and Young, 2001; Downing and Chim, 2004). The asynchronous nature of online discussion rooms also allows time for spell checking and re-reading of messages, and sometimes editing for corrections. This can be of particular use to students for whom English is not their first language. Without the restriction of 'turn taking' in a classroom, students may behave differently online to the way they do in class, and the opportunity to reflect and prepare responses can be valuable:

> The discipline of being obliged to formulate one's ideas, thoughts, reactions and opinions in writing in such a way that their meaning is clear to other people who are not physically present, is of key importance in the majority of educational programmes.
>
> (Kaye, 1989, p. 10)

Since the text of the messages in an online discussion room remain permanently visible, the discussion room itself can be used as a learning resource for students to revisit, enabling them to read and think without the pressure of trying to note everything down as they would in a traditional classroom (Kaye, 1989, p. 12).

Facilitating groups

Becoming an online tutor involves the development of a new range of skills. First, you must become confident in using the technology and then relate to the techniques that need to be adopted when dealing with student groups online. A raft of staff development courses (face-to-face and online) has been developed in offering training for staff as e-moderators and online teachers, and guide-books abound. With regard to the new online moderation skills that you might need to learn, Salmon (1998 and 2000) offers a five-stage model that is designed to support a student-centred approach to learning. She suggests techniques that are useful to teachers to move students' online learning forward through stages of:

- access
- socialisation
- information sharing
- knowledge construction
- independent development.

The design of how your learning tasks are structured and the space you make available for your students will depend on the course and the

79

purpose of the online discussion rooms. It is likely that student skills in using and finding discussion rooms for their course work will improve with practice, so perhaps the most important thing in designing your online tasks is consistency in the way you organise resources.

Student skills for online discussion

It would be unreasonable to expect that all students will be familiar with using online discussion rooms. You may know that your particular group will have been exposed to the use of online discussion rooms in previous modules. If you are not sure of this, it is worth providing support or training for your students:

- be detailed and precise in your instructions;
- clarify to your students the different purposes of email and online discussion;
- provide opportunities (and activities) for students to become familiar with posting and reading messages before linking them to assessed coursework;
- remember, that in the first instance at least, your students may be unconvinced of the benefits of taking part.

It is important to ensure students are clear about **netiquette** or good manners online and about the kind of writing you expect from them. To a certain extent, you can model this for them in the messages you post, but it is also a good idea to set clear guidelines at the start of a programme relating to what kind of behaviour is acceptable and what is not. Will typos and incorrect grammar be tolerated in the interest of getting thoughts coming thick and fast? How will you discourage students from simply adding 'me too' or 'I agree' after the first well thought-out post?

There are many reasons why participation may be slow in an online discussion room, but you should be prepared to be proactive in encouraging discussion. Paulsen (1995) describes a range of techniques for structuring 'many-to-many' discussion rooms, including debates, role plays, buzz groups, etc. Online discussions, like on land discussions, work best if they are focused, specific and time-bound, with clear aims and outcomes:

One of the first duties of an online tutor is to 'set the agenda' for the conference: the objectives of the discussion, the timetable, procedural rules and decision-making norms. Managing the inter-actions with strong leadership and direction is considered a sine qua non of successful conferencing [. . .] Just as in a face-to-face course, the online tutor needs to let students know what to expect, what are the requirements of the course, the activities and the schedule.

(Mason, 1991)

Deciding on the purpose of a discussion room is part of your learning design decision process. Depending on the nature of the learning task, you can create one room for a large group to work in over a period of several weeks or months, or much more focused small rooms for small groups or individual tasks. For each room you should consider:

- Why will this room be useful for my students' learning?
- What do I want my students to do in this room?
- When will they use it?
- Where should it be positioned?
- Who should have access to it?
- How long should it stay open for contributions?
- What will happen to the room (and the messages) at the end of the task?
- What will my role be in monitoring, reading or replying to messages?

PLANNING INDIVIDUAL SESSIONS – LESSON PLANNING

Having looked more broadly at what the various teaching and learning methods can achieve – and we hope that you have reflected on the methods you have experienced and how effective (or not) they were in supporting your learning – we now move on to Gagné and Briggs' (1979) 'events of instruction'. This can be applied both to teaching and learning methods in general, and to a particular class or series of sessions that you have to plan. After the list of the *events* (originally there were nine but we have condensed them to eight), we will consider each in turn and see how it might be applied to the session planning process:

1   gaining attention;
2   sharing learning outcomes;
3   eliciting existing knowledge/experience;

4   providing new 'material' as a quality learning experience;
5   engaging the learner in related tasks;
6   providing feedback on performance;
7   assessing the value added;
8   promoting 'deep learning'.

Gaining attention

Your students are likely to arrive at your session from a range of other activities, classes or work. How do you focus them on the topic of your class and the learning that is to be achieved? How do you motivate them to stop thinking about food; the essay they are planning; their boy- or girl-friend; their need to get to the library; the party tonight, and to concentrate on you and the topic of the class? 'Shall we begin . . .' might indicate your readiness to start but not necessarily theirs. This may be enough to settle the group and stop them talking, but more is needed to gain their attention. Try starting with:

- a question (that may be answered during the session) or a challenge
- a picture or a diagram that represents or visualises some aspect of the content
- a quote, to surprise or that challenges conventional thinking – read it out or project through an OHP or PowerPoint
- an application of the theoretical input that sets the planned content in the real world
- a short video clip
- a brief extract of music
- a current newspaper headline.

All the above are designed to capture thinking and focus attention. Starting by telling the students what they can gain from the session can work also, but it has to be done with flair and interest on your part.

Sharing outcomes

It is sometimes suggested that we should begin a class with a list of the intended learning outcomes, perhaps projected as an OHP slide or on PowerPoint. This does the job of telling the students the planned outcomes, but can be rather dull and is unlikely to spark interest. A better way would be to talk about the content and process of the class as they relate to the outcomes in order to show the coherence of what they will be doing and what they should be gaining from it. Using a second projector in order to leave the outcomes in view throughout the class and enable you to refer to them on occasion (assuming that you are using the 'first' projector to give content/activities) is an effective method, particularly for complex ideas or classes where there is a lot of activity and examples that may obscure the purposes. This keeps the focus on the learning rather than on the detail of the examples and illustrations. When a number of classes are being used to develop a particular skill or understanding, it may not be appropriate to start each session with the same list of outcomes. You need to be more creative in the way that you link sessions and remind students of the purposes. Remember, the whole point of learning outcomes is to provide a framework or scaffolding for the students' learning. And, of course, don't forget at the end of the class to review progress against what you said at the start.

Eliciting existing knowledge/experience

'Please write down all of the words and ideas that come to mind when I say **reaction kinetics/mitosis/Jane Eyre/the assassination of John F. Kennedy**' can give you a quick indication of what is known on a topic. Furious writing or blank stares and blank pages tells all. Depending on the response, you might decide to talk through what they have written, or brainstorm a list as a whole group, or just leave it as a way of getting students to start thinking. The latter might save time, but does not pick up the muddled or incorrect thinking – which is not the ideal foundation on which to start building. Alternatively, you could give a list of words and ask students to 'vote' (a quick show of hands) to say whether they have heard of the idea/word and if they know what it means. Alternatively, a content or concept map (see Chapter 4) of the topics that have and will be covered can act as a reminder of where the class have been, are currently, and are going. Or simply a brief reminder of what was covered in the last class or two can suffice, but this has the disadvantage that it is eliciting your memories and not those of the students.

Some staff make use of electronic classroom voting systems to elicit more detail than a traditional show of hands. An electronic classroom voting or personal response system can be used in conjunction with overhead slides or PowerPoint to create and show instant bar charts of student responses. Used at the start of a lecture or seminar, this can engage the whole class in a discussion of why differing views might be held on specific topics. For example, in an introductory lecture about the copyright issues surrounding using, copying, distributing and republishing material and images found on the Web, students were offered a number of scenarios to consider and asked to decide whether the protagonist is contravening copyright law. The students considered all the scenarios for about ten minutes on their own, and were then asked to vote publicly on each. Web copyright and sharing of files is an area where many people hold conflicting views of what is right and wrong. The use of the e-voting system resulted in a lively (and lengthy) discussion around the scenarios and exploration among the group of shared assumptions and knowledge of licences and law. The session was mentioned specifically by students in the module feedback.

Providing new 'material' as a quality learning experience

New material needs to be structured and sequenced in order that it makes better sense to the students, and you need to think about how much the students need. What is the best use of their **quality time** with you – your telling them information that they could as easily read and understand from a book or handout, or explaining and working with them to resolve the really hard aspects that you know they will find difficult to understand? You need to think about providing a framework that gives the essential aspects only, that is clear and well understood. Then it is their task to broaden and deepen their knowledge and understanding by reference to the materials, literature, readings, etc., that you direct them to. And they need to be told this.

A quality learning experience incorporates a range of aspects, but the three priorities are:

- appropriate level:
  - demanding and challenging, but not beyond them;
- reasonable rate:
  - what you can deal with in a ten-minute period, the best students can probably deal with a little less;
  - this is not only information rate but also processing time for group work – the time needed to complete activities either individually or in groups;

■   the necessary learning resources:
     – being available and in sufficient quantity.

In addition to a growing wealth of e-books and e-journals, web searching is becoming an increasingly popular method among students for researching and broadening their knowledge on a topic. Since we all know that basic web searches return materials of varying quality, it may be in your interest to give students pointers to steer them towards materials of the quality required for studying on your module. One way to do this is to select specific sites and recommend them by including links and references in your materials and reading lists. When you recommend a site you are giving it your stamp of approval, so take a good look at it. When looking at a site, you can make decisions about whether you want to recommend it, based on the following evaluation criteria adapted from Cameron (2001):

■   accuracy
■   authority
■   objectivity
■   currency
■   coverage
■   copyright.

Accuracy If the site covers material in your subject area, you are probably in the best position to judge its accuracy. Many people (not just students) tend to believe that if it is on the Web, it must be true. If a website is made with an eye to detail and accuracy, it will usually include the name or contact details of the author (often at the bottom of the page). If there is no name, it is unlikely that anyone is taking responsibility for the information. Many sites also include information about the aims of the site and the organisation behind it.

Authority Authority on a subject is often hard to determine. Since anyone can publish on the Web, there may be many instances when the people most qualified to comment on something are not sanctioned by any traditionally recognised institution, but there are some things you can look out for to gauge where information is coming from. Is the author qualified or an expert on this topic? Where is the site hosted? You can draw some conclusions about where a site is hosted by its URL. Is it in an educational institution, e.g. ac.uk or .edu, or any official domain, e.g. .gov, or a commercial organisation, e.g. .com, .co.uk, .net? Watch out for free hosting services such as msm, yahoo, freeserve. You can also sometimes spot the country of origin. United States URLs do not incorporate the .us, but other countries will always include the .xx code, e.g. Australia .au, Japan .jp, Italy .it

Objectivity Bias is not necessarily a bad thing. Many published academics have biases, even if they deny it, and some even base a career on it. Bias does not mean that a site is worthless, but students should be wary of accepting information at face value. The judgement you make about the objectivity of a website is similar to the judgement you make about a dubious academic article – it comes down to your own common sense. Look carefully at any sponsorship on a page.

Currency Many websites are out of date or abandoned – once they are put up they are forgotten and never taken down. Other sites contain information that doesn't need to be updated – depending on the subject, this may not matter.

Coverage If you are thinking of expanding your students' reading beyond topics usually covered in books and journal articles, the Web covers a whole new range of topics. There is a lot of rubbish on the Web, but there are also some gems and you may want to recommend sites which seem very amateurish simply for the coverage and focus they have. Remember, though, sites maintained by individuals for their own use are often moved, changed or deleted by their owner and they will not alert you of the change. You should check these links regularly.

Copyright Nowadays, most reputable websites, particularly those that contain desirable academic resources, will include some kind of copyright information or 'terms of use'. You will often find that information linked from the front or home page. Just because it is on the Web doesn't mean it is copyright free. If copyright information is available, it will say so. If a site contains images or resources that you are tempted to take and copy, and there is no copyright information, you must make reasonable effort to clarify the copyright position.

Engaging the learner in related tasks

Earlier, we mentioned processing and application activities. The former allows the student opportunity to come to terms with the ideas, check out meanings and resolve questions and, through individual and group work, begin to take ownership of the concepts and ideas. The latter enable students to use the ideas and practise skills. It may not be possible to achieve both in the same session, but explaining what you expect your students to do in class and outside, and why it matters, will provide incentive and reassurance that they can be successful.

The notion of taking ownership has come through a range of studies on how students learn. While later research has replicated and reinforced the ideas, the work of Marton *et al.* (1993) with UK undergraduates provides an interesting set of stages of learning. The earlier ones suggest that the ideas belong to others and then, as understanding occurs, there is a change in how things are seen. The six stages are:

- increasing one's knowledge
- memorising and reproducing
- applying
- understanding
- seeing something in a different way
- changing as a person.

If you expect students to practise skills outside class time, it may be worth investigating particular subject-specific software or simulation packages that will give them opportunities to apply the knowledge they have been given, perhaps in simulated real world situations. If you find that you are limited in the amount of discussion you can facilitate with your group during class time, you should think about using online discussion rooms or groups to extend the time for exchange of ideas. Most universities, and certainly those offering a VLE, have the facility to use online discussion rooms in any course. Online discussion rooms provide a way of sending messages to a group, using a discussion forum of threaded messages, rather than email for storage and mediation. All the messages sent to a discussion room appear in one place and students visit the discussion room to access them. Unlike face-to-face discussions, online discussion rooms do not require students to be available at a particular time. For this reason it is often called 'asynchronous'. Some teachers choose to combine new modes of online communication using both asynchronous and synchronous 'real time chat rooms'.

The advantages of using online asynchronous discussion rooms are listed in Table 5.4. As you can see there are some disadvantages too, and these may need some planning for on your part. The important

87

TABLE 5.4 Pros and cons of online, asynchronous discussion

Advantages	Disadvantages
May increase participation	It is usually text-based providing no body language or other visual cues
May increase student involvement	to meaning
Encourages peer tutoring and peer learning	There is inevitably a learning curve so that discussion can be slow to start
Encourages a student-centred approach	Assessing online activity remains problematic
Encourages deep understanding and deep learning	Encouraging active participation can be difficult
Facilitates collaborative work	Managing large volumes of discussion can be time consuming
Makes records of discussions available	It may require tutors to learn new online moderation skills (or adapt their existing skills)

Source: Adapted from J. Seale and Rius-Riu (2001), p. 14.

message here is to think about what we have termed 'processing and application activities', as you are planning the sessions: how the activities will link to planned outcomes and the content, and the stages of the activities before, during and after.

Providing feedback on performance

Formal and detailed individual feedback may not be possible until much later when students have completed and submitted a piece of coursework (that may or may not have credit attached to it). However, it is essential that we provide a range of on-going, informal, formative information to students as we work with them in class. This may be as simple as encouragement to keep going if they are struggling with a concept or problem, evaluating their developing understanding as evidenced by questions and activities in class, asking them questions to gauge their understanding and commenting (constructively) on their answers, by suggesting additional reading. All the informal chat that occurs in the session should be seen as possible feedback opportunities.

Linking online self-assessment tests and quizzes that include feedback in response to students' answers to your course materials can be very effective. For instance, you may find it interesting to design multiple-choice questions that include 'distracter' options in the choices which will draw out common mistakes or misconceptions and then write feedback for students who choose the option which directs them to the course materials that explain that content area.

Assessing the value added

This may be very difficult for you to do within the class, but could be much easier for the students to do for themselves. And this is where the intended learning outcomes for the session become vital, as students can be encouraged to gauge how they think they are achieving the expectations. The difficulty is, of course, that the outcomes may not have levels of achievement built into them, so the students' self-assessment is limited. However, students should be able to decide what extra effort they need to make. With first-year students, it may be helpful to rehearse this process with them during the first few classes so that they start to build it into their thinking. You will be helping them to develop as independent learners if they are able to self-assess their achievements in this way. However, you can only encourage and promote this process – the old adage of taking a horse to water certainly applies in this instance, as despite all your efforts, the horse may decide not to drink.

Promoting 'deep learning'

Deep learning is about connections and meaning rather than focusing on isolated elements and aiming to rote-learn. Deep learning does involve memorising, but memorising for the purpose of long-term understanding, and gaining meaning and significance for the ideas and concepts, rather than memorising for the short-term without necessarily having understanding. Deep learning is usually equated with successful learning that can be built on and developed, whereas surface learning is too short-term to enable progression and linking. The challenge is to be able to achieve the appropriate conditions in all classes – getting the right balance of challenge and support linked to opportunities to process the concepts – and for all the students.

What is so useful about Gagné and Briggs' list is that it reminds us of the essential components of any individual or set of teaching events, and notes the need for a range of methods in order to achieve all the outcomes. We have said that innovation is not synonymous with best, but perhaps variety is. With our eight events in mind, the next stage is to have a means to pull together all the planning for a session in a simple way – a teaching plan.

SESSION PLANS

A session or teaching plan is a summary of your thinking, planning and preparation for a teaching session. In no more than a couple of pages, the plan provides a schema for the class, a place to note down enhancements and changes for next time, and an aide-memoire for when you next deliver the session.

There are a number of ways of producing a session plan. We will consider two – a checklist and a proforma. We will discuss examples of both, but as you read you should be thinking about a format to suit you and the context in which you work.

Alison Cooper (Centre for the Enhancement of Teaching and Learning (CETL), University of Lancaster) suggests the following (not definitive) checklist of things to think about:

1   the first 10 minutes – how to start the session (bearing in mind the 'stragglers') and how to 'warm' it up/get everyone focused;
2   how to share the aims and the intended outcomes of the session;
3   how to link this session with previous and future sessions and any work done outside of sessions, e.g. pre-reading;
4   how to structure the time and vary the activities and pace;
5   how much material can be realistically covered;
6   what to do if you run out of time/materials – contingency plans;
7   what activities the students will be doing;
8   how to get all the students to be actively involved and take some responsibility for the session;
9   how to use questioning;
10   when and how to use resources and equipment;
11   how to use body, voice, space to communicate;
12   how to address any diversity or disability needs;
13   how to identify understanding and address any misunderstanding and difficulty;
14   how to identify what they are taking away from the session, and for the students to know this;

15   what you want them to go away and do next;
16   what the last five minutes will involve and how the session will
      finish.

By briefly answering the questions you have a plan for content, methods
and process in mind. Questions 5 and 6 are well worth spending a little
extra time on if it is the first time that you will be teaching the session.

An alternative is a proforma. The example (Table 5.5) we provide
would run over two pages and the gaps have been removed for the sake
of brevity. The first page has a student focus and asks for information
about the group and the planned outcomes. The second page, best as a
landscape layout to give space, is teacher-focused and provides a timeline for the class. Some colleagues find the idea of giving specific times
problematic, but again this can be very useful if it is the first time that
you will be teaching the session.

TABLE 5.5 A session plan, page 1, student focus

What do you know (assume) about the group?

....

....

Aims of the session

....

....

Learning outcomes to be achieved

....

....

By the end of the session, learners will be better able to . . .

TABLE 5.6 A session plan, page 2, teaching focus

Timeline	Content to be covered	Organisation of group	Teaching/ learning method	Resources	Assessment approach

Lesson plans of this type provide a useful way to ensure that you cover all the topics in the allotted time, and include reminders of all the resources. The document can be used to review the session and jot down plans and alterations for the next time you run it. In addition, if you are planning to use a VLE to support your teaching, you should include this in your teaching plans and in your learning outcomes, making it clear to your students where they will find the computer-based or online materials you are going to expect them to use.

SUMMARY

The important messages from the chapter are variety of approaches and appropriateness of method to planned outcomes and student needs. The next stage in the course design cycle is finding out what students have achieved relative to the planned learning outcomes – assessment. The next chapter deals with this aspect.

Chapter 6

Matching your assessment to outcomes

INTRODUCTION

Assessment plays a crucial role in the curriculum and serves many purposes – for individual students, their teachers and the institution as a whole. As a teacher in higher education, your involvement in assessment is one of the most important and demanding aspects of your work. The role of assessor carries with it a high degree of responsibility in terms of ensuring that the academic standards and integrity of the institution are upheld and that all students are treated fairly and equitably. This chapter will provide you with an opportunity to consider your role in assessing students' work and will examine the basic principles of assessment and the different purposes it has so that you will be able to perform your assessment duties with increased confidence and professionalism. We will focus on the development of an assessment strategy for your course rather than look in detail at the design and marking of individual assessment tasks, as this latter aspect is covered comprehensively in other books in the series. In particular, we will look at the dual role of assessment in promoting and measuring learning and the design of course-assessment strategies that enable both functions to be fulfilled.

ASSESSMENT AND COURSE DESIGN

In the context of course design, assessment should be seen as an essential and intrinsic part of the learning process and not something bolted on to the end of the course as an afterthought, merely to measure the learning **after** it has taken place. Assessment has to be planned into the course at the outset. As Ramsden (2003) has asserted, assessment defines students' curriculum for them, and dictates what they will spend their time on and how they will organise their studies. As pressures on students increase, they may become more and more strategic, and assessment can then determine what and how students learn. Indeed, when we looked at writing learning outcomes in Chapter 3, we suggested that they needed to be SMART – where the 'T' stands for 'testable' – so you might usefully ask the following question **while** writing your learning outcomes: 'How will I know/find out whether this has been achieved?' This already gets you started in formulating an assessment strategy, or alternatively rewriting the learning outcomes.

Assessment is also part of the learning partnership we have with students. It is a feedback loop by which we can gain greater understanding about the effectiveness of our own teaching and as a consequence modify our approach. This also indicates that assessment is part of a two-way learning process and needs to be implemented during learning.

Developing an assessment strategy

In order to develop a strategy for the assessments in your course, you first need to consider exactly **why** it is you are assessing students and examine **what** it is you are assessing. Only then are you in a position to think about **when** that assessment should take place and ultimately to consider the most appropriate method or methods of assessment to use – the **how**. We will start the discussion by examining the reasons for assessment and will then look at precisely what is being assessed by exploring the relationship between assessment and the aims and learning outcomes, and introducing the concept of an **assessment specification grid**. You will need to refer back to the version of the Bloom taxonomy that was introduced in Chapter 3 (see p. 45). We will then look at when assessment might take place, before finally considering the methods that might be used – i.e. this chapter will ask the 'why?', the 'what?', the 'when?' and the 'how?' of assessment.

WHY ASSESS?

In order to design an assessment strategy, you need to be clear about what it is you are trying to achieve. Assessment, as we have already stated, serves a number of purposes for the students, the teachers and the institution as a whole (see Table 6.1). The reason for the 'function' column is to make a distinction between two major purposes of assessment – to support learning and to judge achievement. It is clear from

TABLE 6.1 Purposes of assessment

Purpose	Function
For students, assessment	
Enables them to demonstrate their learning	Supports learning
Enables them to improve their learning and study skills	Supports learning
Acts as a motivating factor by providing a focus for their learning activity with timescales and deadlines to work to	Supports learning
Provides intellectual challenge and can stimulate their interest in and around the subject	Supports learning
Can provide opportunity for students to work collaboratively to achieve a common goal	Supports learning
Ultimately decides the degree classification that they are awarded	Judgement
For staff, assessment	
Provides an opportunity to give constructive and encouraging feedback to students on their learning	Supports learning
Enables them to monitor the effectiveness of their teaching	Supports learning*
Enables them to make decisions about whether students can progress through academic levels	Judgement
Helps them to ultimately decide the degree classifications they award	Judgement
For the institution, assessment	
Assures and upholds the standards of the institution	Quality assurance
Enables the institution to make its results public	External judgement

* by the teacher.

this distinction that your answer to the question 'why assess?' will also affect the answers to the questions of 'when?' and 'how?' to assess and 'who?' will do the assessing.

Summative assessment

Assessment for judgement is termed **summative assessment**, its primary purpose being to measure **the sum of the learning**. It is used to classify students and forms the basis on which qualifications are awarded. The outcomes of qualifications can be used in league tables as perform-ance indicators, and this sends signals to the outside world about the quality of the institution and the 'value' of its qualifications. For the grad-uate, their future can hinge on the degree classification they are awarded as it can have a major impact on the choice of jobs open to them and the further qualifications they may be permitted to study for.

Assessments of this type carry high stakes and as such require accuracy, fairness and consistency in the way they are designed and implemented to ensure that they provide equal opportunities for all our students to demonstrate their achievement and so gain the qualification/ grade commensurate with their potential. The need to follow assessment procedures, such as anonymous marking and second- or double-marking, are important here, as is the need to ensure the security of the assess-ment process and the accurate recording and handling of results. All of these cost, and assessment for judgement is also high stakes in terms of resources, especially staff time. The resource issue is illustrated by the final stages of summative assessment, when degree classifications are being decided. This process is always monitored and moderated by a peer from another institution – an external examiner.

Formative assessment

Assessment for supporting learning is **formative assessment**, which may or may not have a summative function. Formative assessment is assessment that occurs during learning to inform and direct learning. It provides feedback to the student about progression towards a goal or standard and may carry marks, but the principle purpose is development rather than judgement. This type of assessment still takes time. However, the expense of examinations, external examiners and double marking are not necessarily issues, making it less significant in terms of cost.

In the design of your course-assessment strategy, you should ideally be aiming to give summative assessments – assessment for judgement – a formative function through their timing and the provision of feedback. In this way, you can maximise the feedback that students receive and achieve the greatest benefit for the effort expended.

ASSESSMENT TERMINOLOGY

It will have started to become apparent that there is a raft of assessment-related terminology that we need to have a common understanding of.

Some of the more common terms have already been explained and some are defined below: in addition, Knight (2001) gives a more detailed treatment.

Validity of assesment

A valid assessment is one that is appropriate for the ability/attribute being assessed. If you wish to know whether someone can drive a car, a valid assessment would be to require them to drive a car safely, observing the laws and protocols of the road. Writing an essay about driving would not be a valid assessment of their ability to drive or of their driving skill. See Table 6.2 for some examples of valid assessments.

TABLE 6.2 Valid assessments

Outcome	Content/learning	Assessment
A skill	Detailed directions and/or demonstration, followed by opportunity to practise	Observation of student performing the skill
Illustrate theory to give understanding	Appropriate theory Task to do	Short test requiring demonstration and application of theory (probably written)
Writing a report	Report format Practice Access to examples of various reports	Student produces a written report to specification

Ways to improve the validity of assessments

There are several ways in which the validity of assessments can be reviewed and improved:

- ■ Ensure that learning outcomes are written in such a way that they can be assessed.
- ■ Select assessment methods that are appropriate for measuring the learning outcomes.
- ■ Implement a range of assessment methods to add variety to students' learning experience and provide different ways for

students to demonstrate that they have achieved the learning outcomes.

■ Ask your students whether they see congruence between what happens on the course and the assessments they are set.

Reliability of assessments

The term 'reliability' encompasses a range of issues relating to the **objectivity, accuracy and repeatability** of the assessment. One factor that is directly related to these issues is the **consistency of marking** – i.e. by a single marker at different times and between different markers. For example, can you guarantee that you would give the same mark for a student's essay if you marked it at the end of a tiring day (where standards may drift with time), just after you had marked a particularly good or poor essay, when you had marked good work from the same student previously (a possible halo effect), or even just after you had heard your latest research paper had been accepted? Reliability is about whether one applies exactly the same standards and criteria throughout the marking process, both to the same piece of student work at another time and to work of other students in the group. Consistency of marking also relates to whether another examiner would agree with your grades if he or she was asked to mark the same pieces of work.

Reliability also relates to the **accuracy** of the assessment task itself – i.e. whether the outcomes of the assessment are a true indication of the learning and ability of the students being assessed. The desire to be **objective** often means that we assess things that can be easily measured and although this may increase the precision of our judgement, it can over-simplify the assessment to such an extent that more complex, and possibly more authentic, learning qualities are ignored.

An extension of this is that reliability also concerns the **repeatability** of an assessment. Are the procedures robust and consistent enough for you to be certain that differences in the assessment outcomes relate to the differing degrees of learning and ability in the students? For example, if you conducted the same assessment for a similar group of students the following year, you should get a roughly similar range of results.

One of the main ways of enhancing the reliability of assessments is through the use of assessment criteria. These should link directly to the learning outcomes being assessed and, as with learning outcomes, be worded appropriately to the level of study (both of which are discussed later in this chapter).

Ways to improve the reliability of assessments

The following approaches could be used to audit and reflect on the reliability of the assessments that you use:

- Design assessment criteria or a detailed marking scheme at the outset.
- Check that the assessment criteria you are using are congruent with the stated learning outcomes.
- Apply assessment criteria consistently when marking student work.
- Ensure that the assessment conditions are accurate and secure, that data are accurate and handled with care and kept securely, and that opportuities for cheating are minimised.
- Employ anonymous marking, where students names are not recorded on their work to avoid unintentional bias and halo effects.
- Employ methods of marking moderation, where an experienced second marker also marks work to see whether they agree, these include:
  - second marking, where a sample of work is marked by a second marker;
  - double marking, where all work is second marked;
  - a subset of both of the above is 'blind' marking, where in either second marking or double marking, the mark awarded by the first marker is not known by the second.

Transparency of assessments

The transparency of an assessment is how clear it is to students about what is expected and the standards required. This does not mean 'telling students the answers' in advance – e.g. through being over-specific in our criteria – nor does it mean coaching students – e.g. by giving them almost identical questions from previous years' assessments. Improving the transparency means showing students where the goal posts are – i.e. what to aim for – and this can be achieved by providing clear and accurate information to students before they undertake an assessment task.

Ways to improve the transparency of assessments

There are a number of ways in which students can be informed about the assessment process and the standards that they will be measured against:

- develop broad statements giving guidance on general expectations – such as assessment criteria, grade descriptors, guidance notes – and which indicate what constitutes both satisfactory and unacceptable performance;
- provide accurate information to students about their assessments written in a clear, jargon-free manner:
  - indicate how long students should spend on an assessment (e.g. through credit-rating or word limits);
  - indicate the relative weightings of different elements of an assessment to enable students to place appropriate emphasis and effort;
  - state deadlines and any penalties for late submission;
  - indicate when and in what form feedback will be given;
  - give guidance on academic writing – e.g. essay or report writing;
  - provide access to assessment regulations, exam practices and information about what constitutes cheating and/or plagiarism;
- publish the above before students undertake the work and ensure that it is made available in a range of formats:
  - written assignment briefings
  - course handbooks
  - on the Web or VLE
  - verbally in class (although this should be used only to supplement written forms of information and guidance).

You should ensure that you build time into your course to discuss assessments with students and respond to any questions they may have, either face-to-face or virtually through the use of discussion rooms, which will assist transparency. Table 6.3 provides an example of grade descriptors or assessment criteria that can be used to give general guidance about expectations.

WHAT ARE WE ASSESSING?

Promoting deep learning

Within our model of course design, which emphasised the notion of alignment, the aim of an assessment strategy should be to select assessment methods and design assessment tasks that align with the stated

▓ TABLE 6.3 Grade descriptors

Mark	Class or grade	Examination – essay questions
90–100%	First class	Outstanding answer. Unequivocal evidence of originality. Explicit evidence of extensive reading, abstracted and integrated to inform answer.
80–89%	First class	Exceptional answer in terms of structure and content. Critical appraisal of literature and data. Some original material. Well defined arguments presented. Thorough consideration of all dominant and associated issues.
70–79%	First class	Perceptive answer incorporating all dominant issues. Logical development of arguments that are all supported by relevant literature. Evidence of extensive reading. Synthesis of relevant aspects of literature. Lucid presentation.
60–69%	Upper second	Accurate, structured and coherent answer. Most of the dominant issues discussed. Clear development of arguments. Literature used to support some arguments. Limited critical analysis.
50–59%	Lower second	Answer correct but not comprehensive. Superficial treatment of subject. Some arguments presented but not developed. Breadth and depth lacking. Some small factual errors. Very limited reading. Competent writing.
40–49%	Third class	Poorly structured, ill-defined answer. Descriptive approach. Conceptual and factual errors. Insufficient detail. Little evidence of reading.
30–39%	Fail	Essay question not adhered to. Answer unstructured. Significant proportion of answer irrelevant. Lack of coherency. Limited understanding of topic.
20–29%	Fail	Incomplete answer, much material irrelevant or incorrect. Limited attempt to answer question. Tendency for repetition and listing of facts. No obvious structure to answer.
10–19%	Fail	Relevant material very limited. Structure vague. Partial attempt to answer questions but information listed and undeveloped.
0–9%	Fail	Question not answered. Fragments of relevant pieces of information incidentally included.

Source: unknown

learning outcomes (**congruence**) and that tell students what is valued. If you wish to promote deep learning, as opposed to surface or strategic (Brown, 2004, p. 32), it is clear that assessment tasks must not give mixed messages to students about the learning that is desired. For example, if we want students to apply their understanding of a topic or to synthesise their learning, we need to ensure that we do not send out signals that remembering and reproducing are required. These signals can be sent out in a number of ways: by the design of our assessment tasks, the way they are implemented, and even subtly by verbal/non-verbal communication on the part of the teacher. Part of course management is making it clear to students, through the nature of the assessment tasks and the associated course documentation, the standards that are expected and the way the work will be marked.

Biggs (1989b) has identified four key elements to good teaching that promote deep learning:

1 **a motivational context** – getting students involved in the selection and planning of learning activities to promote 'ownership' and therefore motivation;
2 **learner activity** – active learning: learning by doing/processing/reflecting/planning, building on learning and making connections;
3 **interaction with others** – discussions in tutorials and seminars, testing out one's views and hearing the views of other students;
4 **a well-structured knowledge base** – bringing in and building on students' existing knowledge and experience.

This was subsequently added to by Biggs and Moore (1993) to include self-monitoring through reflection and the development of metacognitive skills (study skills, learning how to learn). Similarly, Jackson (1997) provides 'Five Postcards on Good Teaching', which suggests that the following are required for teaching that promotes learning:

1 students must be allowed to make **choices** (and allowed to experience the consequence of their choices)
2 the development of **self-evaluation**
3 a **variety** of experiences must be offered
4 planning of a feasible **workload**
5 the encouragement of **feedback**.

All these elements of good practice in promoting deep learning can be applied to the practice of assessment. Assessment methods and tasks should be selected that allow students to:

■ make choices and decisions about their assessments
■ involve them in planning their assessments
■ engage them in activity (e.g. through working with others)
■ contain elements of reflection and self-evaluation (e.g. through self- and peer assessment)
■ provide feedback on their learning
■ give a variety of learning experience.

Linking assessment to learning outcomes

Courses – modules and programmes of study – should be designed around a framework of what you are trying to achieve: the abilities, attributes, skills and attitudes of the graduates of the course articulated via course aims and learning outcomes. Once you have the framework – know what you are trying to achieve – you can select the appropriate content and teaching and learning approaches to fulfil these aspirations, and then choose assessment methods that test whether your students have succeeded.

Assessment specification grid or table

An assessment specification grid or matrix relates learning outcomes to the assessments tasks within a course. This enables a check on how comprehensively the learning outcomes for a section of a course are being covered. Using the table helps to:

■ avoid undue repetition;
■ relate the assessment techniques to the learning outcomes;
■ adjust the weight that is assigned to the various assessments in order to match the importance of the different outcomes;
■ consider who (tutor, self, peer) might be best placed to assess a particular attribute or ability;
■ use congruent assessment methods.

Table 6.4 assumes a clean slate, and allows the design of the assessment process to match the outcomes and satisfy your views of relative

■ TABLE 6.4 Assessment specification table for a new course

Assessments	Learning outcomes						Totals
	A	B	C	D	E	F	
Assignment 1							
Assignment 2							
Assignment 3							
Assignment *n*							
Examination							
Totals							100

importance of the content and skills. An example is then given for an existing course, which shows how the specification grid was used to make changes to provide a more reliable, valid and practical assessment scheme for the course. The column on the left lists all the formal assessments that occur within the course. This could include assessments that the students are required to do but do not count towards the overall grade. Such asessments provide students with opportunities to develop and demonstrate an ability or attribute. The column of boxes on the far right of the grid is used to give total weightings for each assessment. The row of boxes at the foot of the grid is used to signify relative weightings (importance) of each learning outcome. Both sets of weighting should add up to 100. The boxes in the body of the table are used to assign the value of each learning outcome as measured by the different assignments. As this is not an exact science, multiples of five and ten are usually used to show the relative weightings. It should be remembered that it is not necessary to assess all the learning outcomes for a particular course, as these may be contributing to other courses or being assessed in other courses. Before we look at a particular example, a word about owner- ship. The grid is a course design tool and checks the coverage and appropriateness of assessments, and as such is not really for student con- sumption. It could be misunderstood and misused by students to guide

TABLE 6.5 Assessment specification table for a course

Assessments	Learning outcomes						Totals
	A	B	C	D	E	F	
Assignment 1	5	5					10
Assignment 2		5		15			20
Assignment 3				15	5		20
Examination	5	10		5	15	15	50
Totals	10	20		35	20	15	100

(strategic) learning, as the grid does not show whether assessments must be passed in order to pass the course.

A specification grid was used to assist in the redesign of the assessment strategy for a course in the School of Computing, University of Leeds to ensure that it was aligned with both the learning outcomes and the relative importance of the different aspects of the course. Table 6.5 shows the spread of weightings for an existing module. When analysed using a specifications grid, seven major points arose:

1 Learning outcome C is not assessed: should it be?
2 Learning outcomes B and D are assessed three times each. Given the overall weighting of D (35) this may be appropriate, but the overall weighting of B (20) suggests over-assessing.
3 Learning outcome F is only assessed once. This may be appropriate if the work is near the end of the module and/or given the weighting (15).
4 Are the relative weightings of the four assignments (10, 20, 20, 50) appropriate?
5 Are the relative weightings of the learning outcomes appropriate?

The next two points take us into the realm of 'assessed how?' and 'who assesses?':

6 The examination seems to have only one format. Is this appropriate for all the learning outcomes?

7 Does all the marking have to be done by the tutor? The grid suggests a heavy workload.

Overall, this grid suggests an assessment scheme that has evolved rather than been planned. The assessment schedule was redesigned (see Table 6.6) to reflect more accurately the learning outcomes and expectations. The changes made to the assessment strategy were that:

1 In this instance, all learning outcomes needed to be assessed.

2 Learning outcomes B and D are now only assessed twice.

3 Learning outcome F can only be assessed, practicably, once, given the time constraints. The weighting has been changed as this is a very important topic.

4 The relative weightings of the assessments better reflect their importance, the stage in the course they are set and the expected students' workload.

5 The relative weighting of the learning outcomes are now related to their difficulty and significance.

TABLE 6.6 Revised assessment specification table for a course

Assessments	Learning outcomes						Totals
	A	B	C	D	E	F	
Assignment 1	5	Peer 10					15
Assignment 2			Self 10	5			15
Assignment 3				10	5		15
Examination		5	5		5 15	5 20	20 35
Totals	5	15	15	15	25	25	100

6 The examination now has multiple choice and essay question components. The question types match the objectives **and** marking time has been reduced.

7 Learning outcomes A and D are removed from the examination as they were appropriately tested elsewhere.

8 A degree of self- and peer assessment has been introduced in order to develop students' reflective and critical approaches.

These changes have ensured that the assessments are planned, appropriate and practicable.

WHEN TO ASSESS?

Scheduling of assessments

The assessment specification grid has limitations in that it is only two-dimensional and gives no consideration to the timing of assessments. The quantity and timing of assessments can have a huge impact on the assessments' ability to promote and support deep learning. In UK Higher Education, the creation of a modular system and an academic calendar that is often divided into two semesters mean that assessments have been squeezed into smaller study units that are completed over shorter periods of time. The tendency is to have two summative assessment or examination periods – the first in December or January and then again in May or June – with perhaps one, two (or even more) smaller, either formative or summative in-semester assessment opportunities in between. This, together with the increase in student numbers, has led to a largely over-loaded assessment schedule that is becoming increasingly unmanageable for both students and teachers. Factors in course design that can lead students to take a surface approach to learning are:

■ assessment over-load – too many assessments;

■ bunching of assessments – where too many assessment deadlines occur simultaneously;

■ when there is no choice about the subject or mode of study.

From this, it is apparent that it is not just the way a task is designed, but the **context** that influences a student's approach to assessment. You will therefore need to ensure when designing the assessment schedule for your own course that you do not consider it in isolation, but consult

107

with the overall course leader in order to avoid bunching of assessment deadlines from different modules or units.

The Quality Assurance Agency's Code of Practice on the assessment of students (QAA, 2000b) recommends 'exercising due economy in the number of assessments' and 'ensuring students have adequate time to reflect on learning before being assessed'. The possibility of combining modules and their assessments is also suggested as this creates larger units of study with the possibility of having fewer assessment tasks. This also provides an opportunity for students to make links between topics that would have otherwise been taught separately and thereby synthesise their learning. However, the possibility of combining modules may be outside your control.

The first-year experience

Yorke (1999) considers that, in the case of first-year students, summative assessments at the end of the first semester place too great a burden on students to achieve the required academic standard in the short time since they have started a course in higher education. This is particularly true where students are unfamiliar with the UK higher education system and the nature of study at that level – e.g. students who have come from overseas or who are from families where there is no previous experience of HE. In many cases, these assessments do not contribute to the overall degree classification but simply need to be passed in order to proceed to the next stage of study. You may need to consider the timing and relative weighting of assessments in the first semester of the first year to give students time to adjust before they are assessed, although, again, this may be outside your control. For example, it may be possible to have a small number of formative assessments (or summative assessments of low weighting) that are designed to familiarise students with the academic standards and expectations before any major summative assessment. Again, you could discuss this with the course leader.

Timing of assessments

At the start of this chapter we examined some of the reasons for assessing students and defined some of the terminology. In terms of timing, the rationale for the assessment, the 'why?', will in large part dictate the 'when?' and this may fall into one or more of the following categories:

- **Diagnostic assessment** – which provides an indicator of a learner's aptitude and preparedness for a programme of study and identifies possible learning problems (and comes **before** embarking on a learning process).
- **Formative assessment** – which is designed to provide learners with feedback on progress and inform development, but does not contribute to the overall assessment (and occurs **during** a learning process).
- **Summative assessment** – which provides a measure of achievement or failure made in respect of a learner's performance in relation to the intended learning outcomes and programme of study (and would come **at the end** of a learning process).

An assessment can involve more than one of the above elements – e.g. a piece of coursework may be formative in that it provides an opportunity for students to be given feedback on their level of attainment, but it also counts towards the module mark and thereby results in a summative judgement on the level of attainment the student has reached. It is also possible for formative and summative assessments to have a diagnostic function in assessing a student's preparedness for further study.

DESIGNING OPPORTUNITIES FOR PROVIDING FEEDBACK

Fundamental to the ability of assessment to support student learning is the provision of feedback to students about their learning and this should in large part dictate the quantity, timing and frequency of assessment tasks within a course. You will need to consider the scheduling of assessment to allow adequate time:

- **before** assessment commences – to give students time to reflect on their learning before they are assessed;
- **between** assessments to give staff time to provide good quality feedback;
- **after** assessment to give students time to digest the feedback, and enable improvements to be made on the basis of that feedback, before submitting further work.

109

The quality of student feedback is an issue raised year after year on student satisfaction surveys, at both national (via the National Student Survey) and course levels, and via institutional audit and subject review processes.

The main issues raised in the National Student Survey relate to the

- **timeliness** of feedback;
- **quantity** and **quality** of feedback;
- **effectiveness** of feedback – the extent to which it is able to inform learning and development.

It should be clear from this that, as part of your course design, you need to develop a **feedback strategy** – i.e. that designs in, from the outset, opportunities for students to gain feedback on their work. This may be achieved through diagnostic, formative or summative assessment, and either through yourself as assessor or through students' own self- or peer assessment. As a word of caution, both Atkins (1995) and Brown *et al.* (1997) suggest that formative feedback on coursework ceases to be of value when it is combined with summative assessment.

NATIONAL STUDENT SURVEY: QUESTIONS ON ASSESSMENT AND FEEDBACK

The questions asked on the recent National Student Survey regarding assessment and feedback were:

1 The criteria used in marking have been clear in advance.

2 Assessment arrangements and marking have been fair.

3 Feedback on my work has been prompt.

4 I have received detailed comments on my work.

5 Feedback on my work has helped me clarify things I did not understand.

In all but two UK HEIs that took part in this survey these questions had an overall satisfaction level of below 4 (out of 5) and this was generally the least satisfactory aspect of students' courses.

National Student Survey, 2005 (www.hefce.ac.uk/learning/nss/)

Policies on giving feedback

As part of enhancing the reliability of assessment you should ensure that all feedback is given in direct relation to the assessment criteria by which work is being judged. This, in turn, should relate directly to the learning outcomes being assessed. In addition, you should help to ensure the transparency of the assessment(s) by indicating to students **when** and **in what form** they can expect feedback on their work. You may find that your school/department or institution has a policy on the provision of feedback and the return of coursework (see the example below) and you should familiarise yourself with this when designing your assessment and feedback strategy.

EXAMPLE: EXTRACT FROM SCHOOL POLICY ON ASSESSMENT

- The policy for deadlines is 9am. If an alternative time is required this should first be discussed with the Director of Learning and Teaching.

- Coursework deadlines should not be scheduled for completion:
  - after the end of Week 11
  - during the half-term
  - after the April vacation (Level 3 only).

- The expected return date for marked coursework is **2 weeks** from the due date.

- The coursework schedule is published to the students via their individual web pages. It displays the issue date, due date and time, and expected return date for each piece of coursework.

Stuart Roberts, School of Computing,
University of Leeds

You may also find that your school/department has a set of assessment criteria for use with particular types of assessed work and you should make sure you find out whether this is the case and use those recommended as appropriate. If this is not the case you may wish to look at Price and Rust (2004) for inspiration.

TABLE 6.7 Methods of giving feedback

Method	Pros and cons
Hand-written comments on work	Personal and individual feedback indicated in appropriate places directly on student work
	Can be time-consuming and repetitive, and legibility and quality may deteriorate over large numbers of assessments
Word-processed comments – e.g. on a front sheet accompanying work	Quality, consistency and legibility can be maintained for all work. Can build up a databank of comments.
	Can feel impersonal and comments are divorced from the students' work
Assignment feedback sheet – ticks or written feedback on a pre-prepared front sheet that ideally relates to assessment criteria	Efficient way of providing feedback to large numbers in direct relation to assessment criteria
	Can feel impersonal
Statement banks – coded letters on work, with the codes corresponding to errors made frequently by students and an accompanying explanation of each code	Efficient and can be further automated through the use of technology
	Can feel impersonal
Model answers	Only of benefit if the student works through their own work to identify mistakes and corrections needed
	Feedback not given in relation to an individual's own performance
Assessment summary sheet providing details of and corrections for the most common errors	Useful for giving feedback on examinations and for guidance to students in subsequent years
Verbal feedback to individual students	No written record, so should only be used to supplement written feedback
Verbal feedback to groups of students – e.g. in a lecture or tutorial	As above, and students can learn about and from the mistakes of others
Electronic feedback: – computer-based – e.g. via objective testing software – by email, VLE and discussion room	Feedback can be given immediately when included in computer-based objective tests There is potential to automate electronic feedback
Computer-conferencing feedback	Useful for distance or off-campus learners
Peer feedback as part of peer assessment	Students see mistakes others have made and how a range of work can be improved
Feedback to students on their own self-assessment	Feedback can be directed towards students' own concerns and to improve own self-judgement

Methods of giving feedback

Table 6.7 gives examples of the range and types of methods you could use for providing feedback. In view of the large numbers of students you are likely to be dealing with and the corresponding quantity of assessments, you may need to find **effective** and **efficient** methods of giving feedback that do not compromise the quantity and quality of the feedback given.

Effectiveness of feedback

Weaver (2006) has researched students' perceptions of feedback to determine whether they value and understand written feedback given to them by their tutors. The outcomes were that, in order to be effective, comments needed to:

- include both diagnosis and guidance:
  - specific, detailed comments together with suggestions for improvement;
  - plus general advice for future work;
- constructively criticise, even good performances;
- balance positive and negative comments as there is a tendency to focus on the negative;
- relate to assessment criteria:
  - comments linked explicitly to basis for judgement;
  - words to match the mark awarded.

You also need to build in opportunities for returning marked work and providing encouragment for students to engage with the feedback given. This also provides an opportunity to give general verbal feedback so that students can put their own work into context and learn from the mistakes of others.

LINKING LANGUAGE TO LEVEL

In Chapter 2, we talked about 'level descriptors'. These are, in effect, sets of generic learning outcomes for study at different levels. You might like to look at the UK's Quality Assurance Agency Qualifications Framework for Honours Degrees in England, Wales and Northern Ireland (QAA (2001)) to see what these might look like in practice. Some HEIs may have developed their own descriptors for studies at different levels within their degree programmes and you should check whether your institution has its own.

As we have said already, we need to write the learning outcomes for our course to be in accordance with the general expectations for that level. Similarly, the nature of the assessment tasks set, the language used to describe them and the standard applied to their marking must also be in accordance with expectations at that level. For example, in practice you would not expect first-year undergraduates to be able to demonstrate the ability to 'critically evaluate arguments, assumptions, abstract concepts and data' in their subject or to make decisions in complex or unpredictable situations. Nor would you expect many honours graduates, outside of creative disciplines such as fine art, design and architecture, to demonstrate originality or innovation. You therefore need to be clear about what you expect your students to be able to do and then set assessments that are appropriate to measure that ability. You then need to indicate to students the level of performance that is expected of them through the guidance that you give and the design of the assessment criteria.

Opposite is an extract from assessment criteria for essay-based assessments in the Department of Spanish and Portuguese, University of Leeds. Assessment criteria were written for four areas:

- relevance to question;
- analysis;
- content (secondary reading/research);
- presentation (structure, referencing).

The assessment criteria for analysis are shown in Table 6.8, which illustrates distinctions between expectations at different levels of study.

HOW TO ASSESS?

Assessment tasks within a course need to link to and build on each other so that students have the opportunity to improve and demonstrate the enhancement in their learning, thereby improving their grades. Designing assessment tasks that build on each other does not mean setting the same type of assessment over and over again. What is required is **variety** in the assessment methods that are chosen so that all students are given the opportunity to demonstrate their abilities in a range of

TABLE 6.8 Matching assessment criteria to level

Grade	Analysis
	Level 1: Definition of key terms and concepts Level 2: Cogent presentation of others' arguments Level 3: Independence of argument
First class	Clear understanding of key concepts/terms and their implications (all levels) Analytical discrimination (especially at L3) Accurate and lucid account of others' arguments (L2) Ability to initiate/sustain independent argument (L3) Ability to formulate and manipulate complex ideas (L3)
2(1) band	Some evidence of analytical discrimination (L1) Ability to sustain a progressive argument Generally accurate understanding of key concepts or terms and their implications Some independent argument (L3) Reasonably lucid account of others' arguments (L2)
2(2) band	Preponderance of description/narrative over analytical discrimination Little evidence of progressive/ coherent argument (especially at L1) Some vagueness/ misunderstanding of key concepts or terms and their implications Argument often derivative (especially at L2/3) Some vagueness/misunderstanding of others' arguments (especially at L1)
Third class	Little or no evidence of analytical discrimination/largely descriptive Argument that is not sustained/ progressive and/ or is often incoherent Some important misunderstandings of key concepts/terms and their implications An argument that is largely derivative (especially at L2/3) Some important misunderstandings of others' arguments
Failed work	Little or no evidence of analytical discrimination (especially at L2/3) Argument that is generally incoherent Misunderstandings of many crucial concepts/terms and their implications Argument that is wholly/very largely derivative (especially at L2/3) Several major misunderstandings of others' arguments (especially at L1)

ways. This variety needs to be considered in relation to the course or programme as a whole and does not necessarily mean, for example, packing many different types of assessment into a single module or unit, as variety in assessment should not result in over-assessment. Of primary concern for you is to design a set of **valid** assessment tasks that are congruent with the learning outcomes and measure what is intended.

Table 6.9 gives examples of a variety of assessment methods and what each might measure. It is worth considering what various assessment tasks actually test, and then decide whether the methods that you currently use measure what you want to be tested. Brown (2001) further analyses these and other methods, and shows how ease and reliability can be improved for each one.

Assessing product versus process

We often assess the 'product' of learning – e.g. a project report, laboratory report, or essay – and not the process that the student has gone through in arriving at that written submission – e.g. searching for literature, planning and executing projects, conducting accurate and professional experimental work. In developing an assessment strategy you need to consider how you can incorporate assessment of 'process'. A major factor in assessing process is devising ways for students to **evidence** their engagement with the learning process (see Table 6.10).

COURSE DESIGN AND PLAGIARISM

An element of assessment that may become apparent during the marking process is that of plagiarism. One definition of plagiarism is the 'copying of ideas, text, data or other work (or any combination thereof) without due acknowledgement'. Enormous pressures are placed on today's university students – e.g. the assessment workload; the pressure to achieve; increased competition in the workplace; plus the need to juggle studies with paid employment. The issue of cheating and plagiarism is taken very seriously in higher education and penalties are generally exercised over those who cheat.

One extreme form of cheating is the purchase of essays from the Web, but many students inadvertently plagiarise because they do not understand how to reference material appropriately. This can be more evident (but not necessarily more prevalent) where students are non-native English speakers. Such students are not confident enough in the language

▓ TABLE 6.9 Examples of assessment methods

Examples	Validity – what each task might assess
Examination (time bound and unseen)	Organising and presenting information, developing an argument, synthesis, analysis, problem solving, writing skills, memory, knowledge, working under pressure, ability to formulate thinking/ideas quickly, revision skills
Course essay or dissertation	Gathering, selecting, synthesising and presenting information, developing an argument, understanding, synthesis, analysis and evaluation, writing skills
Report – e.g. lab report, project report	Organising, presenting and interpreting information, analysis and evaluation, report writing skills
Case study or open problem	Application of knowledge, analysis, problem-solving and evaluative skills
Direct observation and Observed Structured Clinical Exam (OSCE)	Practical or clinical skills, communication skills, working under pressure
Oral presentation	Verbal and non-verbal communication skills, knowledge and understanding, preparing/presenting/structuring information, using visual aids/presentation software, responding to questions
Oral examination	Communication skills, knowledge and understanding, ability to think quickly under pressure
Poster presentation or exhibition – individual or group	Ability to interpret and present findings attractively
Project work – individual/group	Planning, project management, research methods, problem solving, relating concepts to situations, application of knowledge, decision making. Group work – ability to assume certain roles, responsibility to others, team work, leadership
Multiple choice test	Memory, knowledge of subject, ordering of material. Potential to assess analysis, problem solving, evaluation and decision making
Placement	Applying theory, interpersonal/communication/time management/problem solving/technical skills, reflection
Portfolio	Recording progress over time, skills development, self-reflection, analysis, applying theory, organising and presenting material
Video or film	Team work, planning, technical/presentation/editing skills, creativity, decision making
Performance	Self-presentation, team work, pitching material appropriately, selecting material, relating to an audience
Log, diary, minutes	Selection of key issues/elements, reflection, self-awareness, record of process, planning/organisational

Source: Adapted from G. Brown (2001).

TABLE 6.10 Assessing process

Product of learning process	Evidence of learning process
Lab report	Observation of practical skills, e.g.:
	– use of equipment
	– data acquisition and recording
	– team work
	Lab book or instant lab report
Essay writing	Essay plan
	Annotated bibliography
	Hand in draft for formative feedback
Individual project	Project proposal
	Project plan
	Supervision meetings
	Progress reports
	Log book or reflective journal
	Hand in first draft
Group project	As above, plus:
	– minutes of team meetings
	– peer assessment
	– observations of teamwork
	– self-evaluation of team process
Medical diagnosis	Video of diagnosis plus self-evaluation
Design	Portfolio
Your assessment products	How could you obtain evidence about the skills involved in producing the product?

to paraphrase or in their culture it may be considered disrespectful to alter an expert's words.

When implementing your assessment strategy, it is important that you make it absolutely clear what are acceptable and unacceptable forms of citation to all your students and/or that you reinforce what is told to students during their induction or study skills modules. JISC hosts a plagiarism detection service (www.jiscpas.ac.uk) that allows staff or students to upload work to be checked against the Web, essay cheat sites and selected journals. The service provides an 'originality report' which highlights text that has been found elsewhere and provides links to the original source. You may find that your institution already operates this type of detection procedure or you may be interested in trying it out with your students. If students put their own work through this process, they can be sure they have not inadvertently plagiarised before submitting it for assessment.

It is worth saying that essays bought by students via the Web or other means will not necessarily be detected by a plagiarism checker. Many are written 'to order' and are the original work of the writer, even though that may not be the same person who is submitting it for assessment. Where students are resorting to buying essays from other people, there may be issues of workload and time pressure coming into play and you should look across the course to try to avoid several assessment deadlines for different courses falling at the same time.

Strategies for avoiding plagiarism

Detection is not necessarily the answer to deterring plagiarism. As MacDonald-Ross (2004) says 'Prevention is better than cure'. Carroll (2002) shows that there is not one, single approach that will deter plagiarism but a raft of strategies that can be adopted and reinforced. These range from course and assessment design through to how you inform students what is acceptable/unacceptable and finally to detection. In the context of course design, some of the strategies you could adopt to deter plagiarism are:

- To write learning outcomes that encourage students to find out something for themselves through gathering and using information rather than lower order learning tasks such as 'list', 'describe' or 'explain', which invite students to copy from sources that already exist.
- To set individualised tasks in which students are asked to provide individualised answers through exercising a level of choice in the topic – e.g. through selecting and considering a recent event or a famous person.
- To write assessment criteria that reward individuality – e.g. of thought or interpretation.
- To integrate assessments – e.g. subsequent assessments building on the first (e.g. an oral presentation of an essay or project report).
- To ensure that a tracking mechanism is in place – e.g. some work is completed in class (this can be observed); comments are given on draft work/essay plans/literature searches; peer assessment (students judge each other's work against criteria

and are trained to spot plagiarism); signed disclaimers by
students.

■ To assess the process as well as the product – e.g. reflections
on how the group worked in group tasks, individual reflections,
log books.

■ To be very specific in your instructions – e.g. asking
students to refer to two recent book sources and two
Internet sites.

One area that is particularly problematic is collusion, where students
work together and produce almost identical pieces of work. The aim is
to encourage collaboration but to deter collusion. Carroll suggests that
this can be achieved through the assessment of individual work and the
writing of assessment criteria that acknowledge the way in which the
group worked, plus clear instructions to the student about what is
acceptable and unacceptable in terms of collaboration.

USING TECHNOLOGY TO DELIVER AND MANAGE ASSESSMENTS

In response to increasing student numbers, some universities have
invested heavily in computer-based assessment suites both for formative and summative assessments. Students sit tests in computer labs under
examination conditions, and their submissions are collected and authen-
ticated using the institutional information systems. Many more departments have chosen to ask for an electronic copy of assessment submissions
in addition to a paper one, or to provide electronic pigeon-holes into
which students can post their work. (See example on facing page.)

For many people, the use of computers in assessment has been part
of an effort to reduce the time traditionally required from teachers
involved in the process of marking. Whereas you might find it monot-
onous and boring to mark 50 multiple-choice tests by your students, a
computer can do it in seconds. In addition, instead of having to wait
until they next see you for feedback, students can benefit from almost
instantaneous feedback from computer-based assessment systems. A
range of online testing and marking systems are now available and your
institution may well have a licence for one already. As you might suspect,
the search for a computer system that will accurately mark exam scripts
is considered by many to be the ultimate discovery. Although some
success has been achieved in the marking of short-answer, multiple-

---

EXAMPLE: ELECTRONIC SUBMISSION

The School of Biomedical Sciences has decided to require electronic submission of all laboratory reports in future, via the virtual learning environment. This initiative in the school was also linked to another use of technology – the plagiarism detection software already described on p. 118. Collection of scripts electronically enabled staff to batch process them through the copy checker.

University of Leeds

---

choice, fill-in-the-blank, matching- and multiple-answer questions, anything more subjective still requires teacher expertise to mark. That said, computer systems can still have the dual advantages of assisting in the collection and return of assessments, and in broadening the range of ways students can evidence their learning in a wide range of skills.

KEY SKILLS DEVELOPMENT THROUGH ASSESSMENT

Key skills are the skills required to operate effectively in different parts of one's life – e.g. study and employability skills that enable us to be effective in study and work respectively – and are skills that can be applied to new and different situations (formerly they were called 'transferable skills'). Higher education has a role (UK Government HE White Paper, 2003) in developing graduates who have the skills required by employers and in developing a culture of lifelong learning. Lifelong learning is a process whereby individuals return to education throughout their lives to upgrade their skills in order to sustain and enhance their employability. In the UK, the QAA (www.qaa.ac.uk) has commissioned Subject Benchmarking Statements that identify, define and make explicit the general expectations and standards of degrees in a large number of subjects. The statements articulate the attributes and capabilities that graduates of those subjects should be able to demonstrate – generally written in terms of the knowledge and understanding, subject-specific skills, and key/generic/graduate/transferable skills (differently named, depending on which statements you look at) that are required of graduates in the subject. For students to demonstrate those skills, and for institutions to demonstrate that they are being developed by their programmes of study, it is clear that assessment of skills needs to play a role.

121

A key aspect of employability and lifelong learning is the ability of an individual to know what they are good at, to recognise areas that they need to develop, and to understand how to set and achieve goals in those development areas. This is in itself a skill that is often called a **meta-cognitive skill** – learning how to learn – and through this the ability to improve your own learning and performance. Some say that this is the most important key skill.

As we have said, assessment has a role to play in helping students to demonstrate their skills, such as report writing and giving presentations, but it can also be used to help students reflect on and develop those skills through a metacognitive process. In the past, the development of key skills was only ever implicit in the curriculum. Teachers tended to assume that students either arrived with the necessary report-/essay-writing and presentation skills, or that they automatically developed those skills through practising them without ever being taught or shown how to. In recent years, there has been a drive to make key skills development an explicit part of the curriculum, as part of both taught and assessed elements of the curriculum. As we said in Chapter 3, learning outcomes can be written in the cognitive, affective or psychomotor domains. In order to make key skills development explicit, we need to ensure that some of our learning outcomes are written in the psychomotor domain. Programme Specifications then allow us to map the skills development across the entire curriculum to show us where each skill is being developed (see p. 66 for an example).

In order to assess those learning outcomes and hence each of the relevant skills, valid assessment tasks need to be set. Table 6.11 takes the UK's Qualifications and Curriculum Authority (www.qca.org.uk) key skills categories as the initial basis and then, adding more recent notions of key skills, gives examples of possible assessment tasks for each. You may wish to look up the relevant Benchmarking Statements for the subject you teach to see what skills are important to your own discipline, and then consider how you might assess and develop those skills. You should also look to see whether/where they are made explicit within the learning outcomes of the course. If they aren't expressed explicity in the learning outcomes, you may want to make them explicit in your assessment criteria – e.g. allocate a certain percentage of the marks of a laboratory report to the format and presentation of that report.

Incorporating students' use of technology in assessment

When considering the assessments you are designing for your students, you should consider the range of ways in which technology can be used by students in the preparation and presentation of their work. The use of PowerPoint or other graphics packages to produce visual aids for presentations or posters is popular in many universities and as students' web skills increase, many teachers are experimenting with allowing students to create online portfolios of work or websites for assessment.

The use of these new technologies for assessment offers exciting opportunities to think about the skills you are able to assess as part of your course. For example, if you set students a task to create a website instead of a traditional essay, you will still be able to mark their content, but additionally you could include marks and criteria for organisation of information, usability, navigability, use of referenced resources and creativity or design. Since different students have different learning styles and preferences, you may find that different students shine in different styles of assessment. It is important to ensure that any course has a range of types of assessment so as to be inclusive to a diverse group of students.

STUDENT DIVERSITY AND ASSESSMENT

A key concern in assessment is the desire to be fair and equitable in the treatment of students. Students will have a range of learning needs and preferred ways of studying that translate into the way they prefer to be assessed. For example, some students thrive on the pressure of examinations, and like the fact that the assessments are over and done with quickly, and that the mark they get is solely dependent on their own work. Others may dislike the way they have to think and write quickly under exam conditions, and feel that it does not give them a fair chance to express themselves, and that they would perform much better if they were able to do so in their own time. Similarly, some students find having to give an oral presentation an excruciating experience, while others can articulate themselves better in this way and do not like having to write things down. All assessments will disadvantage some students and this can be more so for disabled students. By providing a variety of assessment opportunities, students are given a range of ways in which they can demonstrate their learning. It is more likely that you will hit on approaches that suit individual learning preferences and give students the opportunity to achieve their potential.

■ TABLE 6.11 Assessing key skills

Key skills

Ability – learning outcomes	Possible assessment tasks
Communication	
Taking part in discussions, making presentations, reading and responding to written material, producing written material – essay and report writing	Writing reports, giving presentations, making posters or videos, writing for different media – e.g. journal paper, newspaper article, write a summary, abstract or précis, making web pages
Information technology	
Preparing information Processing and presenting information – e.g. use word-processing, spreadsheet, database and presentation software	Writing reports, using spreadsheets and databases, presenting information graphically, interpreting graphical representations, group work in shared online space making,
Reviewing the use of information technology and specific sofware or tools	Web pages, databases or hypertext bibliographies, making posters or videos
Application of number	
Basic numerical skills, collecting and recording data, working with data – statistics, presenting and interpreting findings – e.g. graphically	Practical skills, using spreadsheets and databases, presenting information graphically, interpreting graphical representations
Working with others	
Working co-operatively, project management – planning and co-ordinating activities, agreeing objectives, working towards identified targets, team roles, interpersonal skills, co-operation, networking and influencing skills, evaluating and improving group work	Group work, group project, assessment of group process – e.g. time management, project management, group dynamics, team roles, leadership, chairing meetings
Problem solving	
Identifying and analysing problems, creating solutions to achieve goals, decision making, planning and reviewing approach to problem solving	Case-studies, computer-based simulations, Objective Structured Clinical Examination (OSCE), design and build projects

TABLE 6.11 (continued)

Key skills

Ability – learning outcomes	Possible assessment tasks
Improving own learning and performance	
Understanding and auditing own learning and study skills (metacognition), skills required for lifelong learning, setting targets and action plans for improvement, following plan to meet targets, time management	Portfolios, progress files, skills audit, professional development plans, reflective writing, self-assessment of own work
Information literacy	
Effective searching and evaluation of information sources, skills in referencing and citation, organising, using and synthesising information, publication of information in various formats	Annotated and hypertext bibliographies, making web pages, contribution to online collections
Intrapreneurship	
Working within an organisation to effect change by developing new ideas, procedures or products, and by innovating practice to enhance the business	Reflecting on work-placement activities – e.g. networking, managing awkward situations, creativity, understanding decision making, negotiation, team working and writing, applying work-based experience to academic study
Entrepreneurship	
Enterprise skills, innovation, invention, creativity, motivation to succeed	Work placements, case studies – e.g. setting up own business – being a company director, design projects and competitions

DISABLED STUDENTS: ASSESSMENT REVIEW CHECKLIST

■ How accessible are the requirements, guidelines and resources for assessments (e.g. assessment documentation detailing deadlines and submission procedures, key texts that support the assessment)?

　　– Are they made available early and in a range of formats?
　　– Have you checked whether the format of assessment documentation meets the needs of any disabled students?

■ What 'reasonable adjustments' can you make to assessments based on, for example, laboratory work, fieldwork and placements, or where there are health and safety considerations?

■ Can you provide alternative ways for students to demonstrate achievement of the learning outcomes? Are there any assessment methods used outside your subject area that could be adapted for use in these circumstances?

■ Can flexible deadlines for coursework be considered to accommodate the needs of disabled students?

■ Can feedback be provided in alternative formats?

■ What are your department/institution's procedures for making special examination arrangements?

■ Is there a designated member of staff who liaises with disability support and examination services?

■ Does the department apply special arrangements to in-class assessments?

■ Where online discussion or computer-based methods are employed as assessments, how can you ensure equity and parity of opportunity?

■ Where self- and/or peer assessments are employed, how can you ensure that disabled students are not discriminated against or disadvantaged? What guidance is given to those undertaking the assessment?

Adapted from Waterfield and West (2002) and Doyle and Robson (2002)

Disabled students and assessment

For disabled students it is not necessarily an issue of choice or preference, but their disability may mean that they are unable to perform certain functions – e.g. walk, see, hear, speak, type, use a mouse, or write/formulate their thinking quickly. This may mean that some students are disadvantaged in assessments that rely on these functions in comparison with others. The Special Educational Needs and Disabilities Act 2001 requires that HEIs as 'responsible bodies' have an 'anticipatory duty' towards the requirements of disabled students and to make 'reasonable adjustments' for those who might otherwise be substantially disadvantaged. The QAA Code of Practice for Students with Disabilities (QAA, 1999b) translates this as 'Assessment and examination policies, practices and procedures should provide disabled students with the same opportunity as their peers to demonstrate the achievement of learning outcomes' (Precept 13).

When developing an assessment strategy for a course and mapping assessments to learning outcomes, it is important to consider at that stage whether the range, loading and timetabling of assessments are suitable for all students and whether any of the methods chosen present particular barriers that could discriminate and disadvantage disabled students. You should also consider whether there are any adjustments that you could make to existing assessment practices that pre-empt the needs of certain disabilities and that would make your assessment practices more inclusive – and this may be of benefit to all students. Providing information about assessments at the start of the course will give students the opportunity to raise any concerns about their ability to undertake them.

WHO SHOULD BE DOING THE ASSESSING?

In the section on promoting deep learning, we suggested that involving students in the assessment process and enabling them to self-evaluate their own performance represents good practice. We have also discussed the need to familiarise students with the academic standards and expectations. These aims can be achieved through assessment strategies that build in opportunity for students to assess their own work and that of their fellow students – self- and peer assessment, respectively. This can be achieved by getting students to:

127

- mark their own and/or each other's work based on a model answer;
- help in the design of the assessment criteria – e.g. by asking them to identify the most important features of a report, essay or presentation;
- self-assess or evaluate their work prior to submission by use of a checklist or prompts so that they can improve their work before submitting it;
- identify aspects of their work that they wish to gain feedback on.

The use of self- and peer assessment helps students to see the way other students have approached the same tasks and also to see the mistakes that others have made. This develops a student's ability to exercise judgement over their own work, which is an important life skill.

 ## FURTHER READING

Brown, G., Bull, J. and Pendlebury, M., 1997. *Assessing Student Learning in Higher Education*. London: Routledge.

Carroll, J., 2002. *A Handbook for Deterring Plagiarism*. Oxford: OCSLD.

Doyle, C. and Robson K., 2002. SENDA Compliance – An Audit and Guidance Tool for Accessible Practice within the Framework of Teaching and Learning. Southwest Academic Network for Disability Supports (SWANDS), University of Plymouth. Available at www.plymouth.ac.uk/assets/SWA/Sendadoc.pdf.

Haines, C., 2004. *Assessing Students' Work: Marking Essays and Reports*. Key Guides for Effective Teaching in Higher Education. London: RoutledgeFalmer.

Waterfield, W. and West B., 2002. SENDA Compliance – An Audit and Guidance Tool for Accessible Practice within the Framework of Teaching and Learning. Southwest Academic Network for Disability Supports (SWANDS), University of Plymouth. Available at www.plymouth.ac.uk/assets/SWA/Sendadoc.pdf

 ## USEFUL WEB RESOURCES

Search the Higher Education Academy (HEA) resources database under 'Assessment' www.heacademy.ac.uk/resources.asp. In particular, look for the Assessment Series of Briefing Papers on the following topics:

1 Yorke, M., 2001. Assessment: A Guide for Senior Managers
2 Mutch, A. and Brown, G., 2001. Assessment: A Guide for Head of Department
3 Brown, G., 2001. Assessment: A Guide for Lecturers
4 Race, P., 2001. Assessment: A Guide for Students
5 Murphy, R., 2001. A Briefing on Key Skills in Higher Education
6 Baume, D., 2001. A Briefing on Assessment of Portfolios
7 Knight, P., 2001. A Briefing on Key Concepts
8 McCarthy, D. and Hurst, A., 2001. A Briefing on Assessing Disabled Students
9 Race, P., 2001. A Briefing on Self, Peer and Group Assessment
10 Stefani, L. and Carroll, J., 2001. A Briefing on Plagiarism
11 Gray, D., 2001. A Briefing on Work-Based Learning
12 Rust, C., 2001. A Briefing on Assessment of Large Groups

Also see what resources are available on assessment practices in your own discipline by looking at the Higher Education Academy Subject Network that is most relevant to your own discipline: www.heacademy.ac.uk/SubjectNetwork. htm

Carroll, J. Deterring Plagiarism in HE: www.brookes.ac.uk/services/ocsd/4_ resources/plagiarism.html

JISC Plagiarism Advisory Service: www.jiscpas.ac.uk

National Council for Graduate Entrepreneurship: www.ncge.org.uk/

Quality Assurance Agency Subject Benchmarking Statements: www.qaa.ac.uk/ academicinfrastructure/benchmark/

SPACE project – Staff–Student Partnership for Assessment Change and Evaluation: www.space.ac.uk/

Chapter 7

Learning materials and resources for diverse learners

INTRODUCTION

Learning materials and resources include visual aids such as handouts and slides/overheads, which include text, diagrams and pictures, plus other media such as audio, video and animations. This chapter considers how you can select and design learning materials that aim to promote and guide student activity both inside and outside formal class contact time – e.g. from information giving, to providing opportunities for students to interact with the materials during a session, to helping students read around the subject, to preparing for tutorials, seminars and assessments. We look at how you might select and design learning materials and resources that support your students' learning – while programme and course management documentation are considered in the following chapter. First, though, we examine the diversity of our students in terms of their learning needs and preferences, and the implications this has on the selection and design of learning materials and resources.

STUDENT LEARNING AND DIVERSITY

Learning needs and preferences

All students are different and students within any cohort will have a wide variety of learning needs and preferences. This diversity of students includes the differences between male and female students, international, mature and part-time students, home students of differing cultural, socio-economic and educational backgrounds, together with students with visible and invisible disabilities. This is in addition to the preferred ways of learning that they may have – e.g. activist, reflector, theorist and pragmatist, as defined by Honey and Mumford's interpretation of the Kolb Learning Cycle (see Brown, 2004) – and the different learning stimuli that they respond to – e.g. VARK: Visual, Aural, Read/Write and Kinesthetic, as defined by Fleming, 2001.

To add to this, as discussed in Chapter 1, many countries around the world are implementing strategies to actively encourage participation in higher education from a broader cross-section of the community. These strategies are particularly aimed at increasing participation by non-traditional students who would not normally have considered higher education as an option open to them. The Government's widening participation agenda in the UK, for example, aims to have 50 per cent of 18–30-year-olds participating in higher education by 2010. In order to achieve this, HEIs are seeking to recruit students from families in lower socio-economic groups and/or where there is no family history of participation in HE.

Similarly, education is becoming more global and students can choose to study in many different parts of the world, such that in any HEI there are increasing numbers of international students (those from outside the home country of the institution), many of whom will have experienced different educational systems and whose first language may not be English.

All these factors indicate that the student body is becoming more diverse and that many students will have come to higher education via different entry routes and may have very different types of entry qualification. The implications of this are that students will come with a wide range of expectations and understanding of the higher education system in which they are to study and with differing degrees of preparedness for study of that nature and at that level. This is not to suggest that the students are 'deficient', but that the learning development process undertaken by each individual will be different as they are all starting from different places – i.e. they will have different learning needs.

Ways of making learning materials that meet different learning needs/preferences

To take diversity of learning needs and preferences into consideration, you need to ensure that you:

- assume that all learning preferences are represented in your student body, so you need to make learning materials available

in a range of formats, to incorporate different learning stimuli such as:
- visual (images, video, multimedia resources, etc.)
- aural (verbal, sound recordings, podcasts, radio, etc.)
- text-based (written materials, books from which to read, etc.)
- kinesthetic (touch, in-class demonstrations, practical work, etc.)

■ enable students to study at different times and in different places that suit them – e.g. where students:
- live away from the university
- have part-time jobs
- have caring responsibilities
- need to revisit learning resources, such as those for whom English is not their first language or who need to access learning resources via assistive technology.

Inclusive resources

Part of your role in selecting and designing learning materials and resources is to ensure that they are **inclusive**. Being inclusive is to do with providing equal opportunities for all students to achieve their full potential and means writing learning materials in a way that speaks to all students, in a language that is familiar and in a manner that does not alienate, discriminate or offend. Inclusivity means not applying stereotypes to students and not assuming that students have the same educational backgrounds, life experiences or cultural reference points as either each other or yourself, the teacher. Student diversity is an opportunity to enrich and internationalise our curriculum and to challenge your own stereotypes and those of your students.

Ways of making learning materials inclusive

To take student diversity into consideration, you need to ensure that learning materials and resources:

■ are written in a clear, jargon-free way appropriate to the level of study;
■ have terminology defined;
■ make clear the expectations on students;

- help students relate their learning to their existing knowledge, prior learning and/or experience – e.g. through context-setting and examples;
- help students to relate the different elements of their course – e.g. by making links between different classes and modules and helping to give a global picture of their programme;
- provide opportunity for students to read around the subject – both to fill in gaps in their learning and to extend their knowledge beyond the topic or level;
- use examples, case studies and problems that include reference to, and have relevance for, both men and women, people from minority ethnic groups and various religions, plus people of different ages and sexuality.

To expand on this last point, you could take examples from around the world, or have case studies and problems that refer to global brands, events or organisations that can provide common cultural reference points. You could even use examples that students are equally unlikely to be familiar with – e.g. an assessment task that takes Antarctica as a case study – in order not to disadvantage students from different cultures. It is also important in subject areas that are heavily gendered (e.g. certain arts and engineering subjects) that your learning materials refer to both 'he' and 'she', while also providing role models for both genders.

Following these guidelines when planning your learning materials will benefit all students and ensure that all feel included and have an equal opportunity to learn. In the broader context of your design of the teaching and learning strategies, Knight and Yorke (2003) suggest that: 'a good learning environment, broadly conceived, contains plenty of opportunities for students to mix, work together on problems, network electronically and construct meanings from a good range of resources' (p. 12).

Accessible resources

This section considers the learning needs of disabled students and how you can make your learning materials **accessible**. This means that learning materials and resources should not present barriers to disabled students. Disabled students should be able to access those resources so that they are able to receive the same learning experience as their peers on the course. In the UK, the Special Educational Needs and Disabilities

Act, which is part of the Disability Discrimination Act (DDA) means that you need to anticipate the learning needs of disabled students and make adjustments to your learning, teaching and assessment strategies to ensure that disabled students are not placed at a disadvantage, in comparison with other students, as a consequence of their disability.

The anticipatory nature of the legislation means that you should not wait until you know that there is a disabled student in the class or registered on the course before making adjustments, as this type of information may not necessarily be declared by the individual or be passed on to all the relevant teaching staff. The legislation is such that if any one person in the institution knows that a student is disabled, then the whole institution is deemed to know.

This is not meant to alarm you as many disabled students will have very specific needs that your department will be notified of and special arrangements made. What we are talking about here are some of the small adjustments to your learning resources that can be made that anticipate the requirements of some disabilities – adjustments that are also likely to be of benefit to all your students. For example, the most common student disability is that of dyslexia, an unseen disability that affects the way in which an individual processes information together with the underlying skills they need for reading, writing and spelling (see the British Dyslexia Association (BDA) website for further information). This clearly has implications for the learning materials and resources that you provide and for which reasonable adjustments can be made, irrespective of whether you know of particular dyslexic students being present. We will consider how the learning needs of dyslexic students can be better met in the next sections when we look at the design of handout materials and visual aids, but it is worth noting here that an increased clarity in written materials and visual aids will be of benefit to all students.

Ways of making learning materials and resources accessible

The implications of student disability on the selection and design of learning materials and resources are that you need to:

- assume that students with a range of unseen disabilities are present in the student body and, in particular, ensure that learning materials and resources meet the needs of dyslexic students;

■ make course documentation and learning materials (e.g. course summaries, lecture handouts, bibliographies, key readings) available in advance and in a range of formats – printed and electronic (e.g. via the VLE) – so that students have more time to read and assimilate the information, can prepare in advance for lectures, can listen rather than write and as a result can take a more active part in sessions;

■ enquire of students to ensure that the format of all documents meets their needs.

Assistive software

There are a number of software packages, called assistive software, that have been shown to be useful in supporting students who learn in different ways. There are many ways to integrate graphics, colours and moving images in your handout and presentation materials, and to bring together a range of media on the Web. These are technologies that support diverse learning styles. Additionally, many universities provide software packages that can be used as part of essay preparation, such as tools for creating mindmaps or organising notes. If you have disabled students in your tutor group, they may be using assistive software to access electronic materials. For instance, a student with a visual disability may use magnification tools that enlarge text on a screen. They may also be using 'screen reader', that can convert Web pages to audio or Braille print, or magnify or rearrange content display. Students with mobility difficulties may find it difficult to operate a computer using a mouse or a standard-size keyboard and often make use of adapted equipment.

FITNESS FOR PURPOSE

If you wish to promote deep learning, as opposed to surface or strategic learning (see Brown, 2004), it is clear that learning materials should not give the impression that they contain 'all the information' the learner is expected to 'know'. If this message is implicit in learning materials, this limits in effect the learning to that of reproductive knowledge which, although it may have its place – e.g. for learning terminology and definitions as a foundation for higher levels of learning – it may not be the desired outcome. It is clear that in order to select and design learning

TABLE 7.1 Mapping learning resources to Bloom's taxonomy

Learning outcome	
Teaching and learning activity	Possible resources
Evaluation, synthesis, analysis	
Problem solving	**Specific to activity**
Complex case studies	Outline of complex problem or case
Individual project work	Problem-based learning scenario
Collaborative group working	Project briefing
Essay	Annotated bibliography
Argument, debate (both in-class and online)	Newspaper articles, journal papers
	General
Independent study	Project report-writing guidelines
Research	Essay-writing guidelines
Problem-based learning (PBL)	Referencing guidelines
Application	
Case study (single outcome)	**Specific to activity**
Problem solving (routine)	Outline of case or problem
Laboratory work	Laboratory briefing
	Video
	Demonstration
	General
	Laboratory report-writing guidelines
Comprehension, knowledge	
In-class discussion	Comprehensive or gapped handout
Online discussion	Definition sheets
Independent learning	Glossary of terms
Quizzes and in-class tests	Reading lists
	Self-assessment questions
	MCQ test paper
	In-class voting
	Discussion questions or prompts

136

materials, you have to be clear about their purpose, and the type and level of learning you are trying to promote. Applying the model of constructive alignment, we need to ensure that our learning materials are designed in such a way that they are congruent with the learning outcomes we want the students to achieve.

As we discussed in Chapter 3, learning outcomes set out the knowledge/understanding, the skills (both subject-specific and generic) and attitudes that a successful student is expected to develop during the course. Table 7.1 maps learning resources to Bloom's taxonomy of learning outcomes.

HANDOUT MATERIALS

This section looks specifically at the selection and design of handout materials, while taking the above factors into consideration. Handouts are paper-based or electronic materials given to students before, during or after teaching sessions. Students see handout materials as being the key to their learning. To them, handouts indicate what is important and what may be assessed. They are something that the student owns and can take away with them. They act as a first point of reference when students are preparing for assignments, and are used for revision in preparation for tests and examinations.

In their simplest form, handouts communicate information. This may be appropriate if information giving is their purpose – e.g. course or module handbooks, assignment briefings, etc. But if handouts are to be used as a tool to support active learning, they should be made integral to the learning process by being designed in such a way as to promote activity and interaction with the subject matter and content of the handout. They should also provide a context for learning by helping to make connections in the minds of the learners – between the content and what learners know or have experienced about the subject already, and between different parts of the course or module.

Selecting the type of handouts

Handouts can be used to support many different types of teaching session: lectures, tutorials, problem classes or seminars, practical or laboratory-based classes, etc. In addition, many different types of activity (see Table 7.2) can be fostered through the use of interactive handouts (see Exley and Dennick (2004) for more detailed information about

TABLE 7.2 Uses and benefits of handouts

Types of handouts	Potential uses and benefits
Complete set of notes	Contain a whole lecture topic and save the student having to write it all down
Skeleton notes	Could contain a summary of the key points and enable the student to annotate and personalise the notes
Gapped handouts: – spaces for definitions, formulae etc. – incomplete definitions, formulae etc. – spaces for graphs, diagrams, maps, flow charts etc. – incomplete or unlabelled diagrams, processes, sequences etc. – spaces for answers to problems	Could be used as a focus for activity in the classroom or laboratory by getting students to fill in the blanks during the session by: – being shown the answer by the teacher – observing or recording during a laboratory – noting while watching a video, animation or demonstration – working on a problem
Single sheet or short handout	Could be used to describe a case study, to provide prompts for discussion, for problem setting or for giving quotes or case law references
Bibliography, annotated bibliography or reading list	Indicates a range of appropriate resources that can prompt students to read around the subject or prepare for assignments
Glossary of terms and definitions	Helpful to international students, students with dyslexia and those with different background knowledge
Copies of PowerPoint slides/ overheads: 2, 3, 6 per page with or without space for notes	A slide-by-slide record of the teaching session that can be annotated

designing handout materials for use in lectures). Some of these methods involve incorporating gaps in the handout that the student completes (e.g. during a lecture session, adding labels on a diagram, definitions, answers to questions, etc.) and these give an opportunity for students to personalise their notes. Other methods can be used to promote group work or discussion (e.g. in tutorial/seminar sessions through setting case studies, problems or issues for debate) and could be given out beforehand or made available electronically – by e-mail or via a discussion room or VLE – to encourage students to prepare for the session. In the case of practical or laboratory classes, handouts can be used to prompt students to make and record particular observations or results. In addition, handout materials can include self-assessment questions that allow students to gauge their understanding of the material.

Table 7.2 shows that handouts can support and promote a wide range of teaching and learning activity, and can vary in detail from comprehensive to outline. We have already discussed 'fitness for purpose' on p. 20 and it is clear that you need to select and design handouts that are fit for the learning you are aiming to achieve.

Comprehensive handouts

There are arguments for providing a comprehensive set of notes, as this means that all students have access to the same information irrespective of their ability to take notes, and ensures that those who are absent through ill-health or who have a disability that makes it difficult for them to take notes are not disadvantaged. It also means that students in the session can concentrate on making meaning of the session content rather than just copying it down. There are arguments against this approach, as it can give students the impression that everything they 'need to know' is in the handout. This can have a marked effect on attendance and can influence the approach to learning that a student takes and the nature of the learning that takes place.

Incomplete handouts

The use of gapped handouts also requires students to be given a realistic amount of time in the session to fill in the gaps, which needs to be built into the session plan. This can have a positive influence as it slows down the pace of the session and can give students more time to process information and formulate questions.

139

Bibliography or reading lists

In general, it is good practice to annotate reading lists, particularly early on in a course. This means providing a short description of the text or article which could:

- highlight its relevance/importance to the topic;
- give the perspective of the author;
- state whether essential, background or extension reading;
- indicate whether the reading is equivalent in content to another but written in a different style;
- describe the reading as overview or specific, mainstream or contentious.

In this way, you will introduce your students to the literature, giving them a view of the writers, perspectives, debates and core concepts. Reading lists should:

- **direct** at level 1
- **guide** at level 2
- and **list** at level 3.

In addition, you need to think about the nominal hours of work and indicate how much you expect students to read after each class.

Designing the handouts

In addition to handout type, the selection of font and the design of the layout can have a major influence on students' perceptions of learning materials: their quality and students' interpretation of them, in particular students' identification of what is deemed to be important (see Brown, 2004). When designing a handout, it is important to make clear its purpose. This could be by stating the aims or intended learning outcomes and by providing an abstract or summary of the main points at the start. The opening is also an opportunity to make the links between those particular materials and other aspects of the course – e.g. making links between this week's and last week's lecture, tutorial or laboratory, or links between a lecture and laboratory class or tutorial – and to make links between new material and what students may know already from prior study or experience. Ideally, you should also include a selective list of references to relevant resources that can be used by students who do not have the requisite prior knowledge or by those who wish to read around or ahead. In the case of handouts for individual teaching sessions, it is often more helpful to students if the reading is directed to specific relevant sections of a book rather than to the overall text so that students who need extra background reading know exactly where to look.

As we have already stated at the start of this chapter, you need to consider the diversity of the student body, and try to design materials and resources to meet the learning needs of all students by ensuring that information is presented in a range of formats, and that handout materials are accessible. You may remember from your own learning experiences having trouble reading the detail on complex diagrams or deciphering the key points from overheads with too much text written too small to read. This is still happening now, which brings us to consider another key issue concerning the development of learning materials and resources – how to ensure that all students have equality of learning experience. To do this, you need to consider following the guidelines in Table 7.3 (adapted from Doyle and Robson (2002), and Waterfield and West (2002).

Timing of handouts

Handouts can be provided at various times – at the start, during and at the end of a session, at the start of a module or, say, a week before each session. Providing materials in advance can have benefits for students, as they can prepare for lectures and listen rather than write so that they are able to take a more active part in the session. This is of benefit to all students, but can be particularly so for those with specific learning needs, such as students with a disability, those for whom English is not their first language, those who have limited prior knowledge of the subject, or mature students whose studies may have been some years earlier. All these students may need longer to read the material or may wish to read around the subject in advance of a teaching session.

In addition to making handouts available in advance, making your teaching materials available in electronic formats enables students to select the ways in which they view or print them. This can make a huge difference to some students, so even if your primary mode of delivery of learning materials is on paper, you may want to make your materials available to your students on the Web or by email. If you make use of video, audio, animations or diagrams in your teaching, you should check

TABLE 7.3 Guidelines for designing handouts

Size and style of font
- A minimum of 12 point
- A sans serif font (e.g. Arial) is found to be easier to read in printed matter, but try to use only one font throughout

Line spacing and justification
- Left aligned with a right-ragged edge is better as justified text can alter the word length

Use of white space
- Make sure there is plenty of white space – e.g. between paragraphs and sections, and that where gaps are left there is enough space for students to write adequate notes

Key points and emphasis
- Use **bold** to emphasise key points, as *italics* distorts the words and underlining can make words run together.
- Avoid using colour to convey meaning
- Use subheadings with a simple but consistent numbering system

Colour of paper the handout is printed on
- Matt, pastel-coloured paper is preferable, as glossy paper can cause glare – you could even photocopy different types of handout on to different coloured paper

The need to have both text and images
- This adds visual stimuli and variety, but you need to avoid writing text over diagrams and make sure the images have enough contrast to photocopy clearly and that they are clearly labelled

that a text explanation of the content is available. This has the dual advantage of clarifying the content and being accessible in the event that the video or simulation does not run as planned on a particular machine.

VISUAL AIDS

PowerPoint or similar presentation software is widely available and used in teaching. You will find it installed on most personal computers and on all the student cluster machines. The package is designed to assist you in designing visual aids to accompany your presentation. Good practice with presentation software in learning and teaching depends on using it to substantially change the student experience and to change what students do with that experience.

▨ TABLE 7.4 Good practice in slide design

Size

- It is wise to pay some thought to the distance students may be from the projector – i.e. they may be sitting at the back of a large lecture theatre
- All students may have difficulty reading vast amounts of text on the screen
- Use a font size of at least 24 pt

Text colours

- Do not use colour to convey meaning, as some students may have visual difficulties – e.g. colour blindness for red and green
- Use high-contrast colours
- Mid-tones do not show up well
- Avoid bright red as it shimmers

Backgrounds

- Be aware of background/foreground combinations, as some are very difficult to distinguish for those with visual impairments
- A dark background and light text is best for dark rooms
- A light background and dark text is best for light rooms
- Keep the same background colour throughout the presentation
- Avoid patterned backgrounds behind text

Text font

- Use **bold** to highlight rather than *italics* or <u>underlined</u> (as this can make the words 'run together')
- Be aware of the type of font used – many people find sans serif fonts such as Arial or Comic Sans easier to read
- Blocks of upper case tend to be harder to read compared to lower or mixed case. It is recommended that you use mixed case

Layout

- Use slide layout tools wherever possible
- Do not put too much information on each overhead – 6 bullet points are optimal (see Figure 7.1)
- Use bullets or numbers rather than continuous prose
- Keep lines left justified with ragged right edge
- Use wider spacing between sentences and paragraphs
- Allow only one subject matter per slide

Diagrams

- Diagrams should be accompanied by a printed version
- If you have to use complex diagrams, ensure sufficient colour contrast
- Write alternative text for images and diagrams

Keep it simple

- Only use one or two text colours, one or two font styles, and one or two animation or transition effects
- Use sound effects sparingly, if at all, and make sure they are relevant

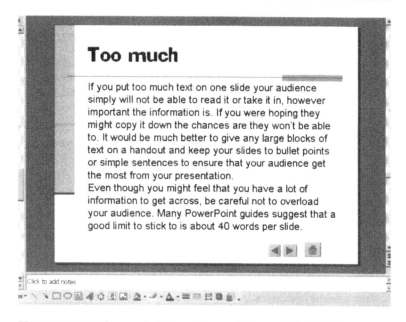

FIGURE 7.1 Screenshot from Microsoft PowerPoint 2002

Preparing a presentation helps you to provide structure and maintain flow. You can emphasise key points and focus attention. If students can read and take notes better, course outcomes can be improved. Having key points, diagrams and terminology clearly presented to them will help students to remember (and spell) more efficiently. Table 7.4 includes a few good rules-of-thumb for preparing PowerPoint slides for projection.

Once you have prepared your presentation using PowerPoint, you have a range of choices in the way you can make handouts available. Handouts of your presentation may help students to structure their notes. If you make your presentation available to them in electronic format, you also give your students options of how they print it or store it for their own preferred study use.

USING WEB-BASED RESOURCES

Presentation software can also sometimes help you to present an idea in a qualitatively different way. It is easy to integrate graphics and animations into your slides, which can illustrate key points and processes for your students. Use images for impact and animations to illustrate a process. Remember to check the copyright permissions (see pp. 146–147) on images before you copy them into your own materials. Images and animations that are free for use in teaching can be found easily if you have good web search skills. A good place to start looking is on the web pages which belong to your university library and Subject Centre. Universities often subscribe to image databases or image banks in which the images have been copyright cleared for use in teaching.

By adding hyper links to your presentation you can bring everything the Web has to offer into your classroom. There are already a wealth of resources on the Web that are relevant for academic study and the ability to link easily to them is one of the most useful features of having a web-based learning environment. It is relatively easy to insert hypertext links into web text and time spent planning will bring dividends. Sometimes, you will be able to discover materials or ideas that the students would not otherwise see. Linking to the Web in lectures allows you to interpret and discuss web-based materials with your students. Select key resources that are integrated into the work they are doing. As well as giving access to new or rare resources, include web links that allow students to 'drill down' into areas of interest. Some teachers find it useful to provide links that include background information on a subject for the student who may be unclear, as well as links to more advanced and detailed information for those who are hungry for more. When you search the Web for resources to use in your classroom, think about using images or video from all over the world. You may be able to find examples from different cultural viewpoints to illustrate your teaching. The Intute Virtual Training Suite tutorials cover evaluating web resources (www.vts.intute.ac.uk). You may choose to assign students to evaluate critically websites or set tasks that involve them in identifying web resources that can be added to your resource base.

USING MULTIMEDIA

The Web is a rich source of audio, video and animations for teaching. These are resources that may be too complex to produce from scratch yourself, so it is worth looking to see if relevant and appropriate resources already exist. Depending on your subject, you may find oral testimonies, great speeches, heart rhythms, music, interviews, performances, educational TV programmes and complex simulations or animations that you can link to or play in class.

145

The key to making good use of this sort of media is to be clear what your students will be doing as they watch or listen. Should they be:

- Answering questions?
- Making notes?
- Annotating diagrams?
- Zooming in?
- Starting and stopping?
- Exploring options?
- Following links?

Before you use a piece of multimedia in your teaching consider the following:

- Which part of your lesson does it relate to?
- How does it fit with the other content of the lesson?
- How will your students know what they are supposed to be doing while they watch it?
- Does the resource need to be interpreted or explained by you?
- What handouts or notes should accompany this piece of multimedia to integrate it into your lesson plan?

COPYRIGHT

Copyright law exists to protect the author of a piece of material from illegal copying of that material. Copyright law applies to text, images, film, maps, diagrams, artwork, photographs, music, computer code, database design – just about anything you can think of, but it is subtly different for each of these and constantly changing both nationally and internationally. Since no one can expect every teacher to be an expert in copyright law, universities and colleges work hard to enable you to use, copy and distribute the materials you need for your teaching materials. You may think that you have free rein to photocopy and hand out sections from any book you find in your university library, or any journal either online or on the shelves that you can find in the catalogue. You do have extensive rights to do this, but these have been negotiated for you by the library from the publishers who own the copyright. In the UK, the licence your university has to permit photocopying of published material has probably been negotiated from the Copyright Licensing Agency (CLA) (see www.cla.co.uk). The CLA licence permits copying in many situations but not all, and you should check your library for information. Many institutions put information on notice boards next to departmental photocopiers. You must also remember that you may be restricted from photocopying large sections of a text or multiple articles from a single journal issue, and that this may vary from journal to journal.

Internationally, copyright law has struggled to keep up with the development of new technology and you should remember that where you may have permission to photocopy a journal article, you should not assume that that permission extends to scanning it. Where you have permission to distribute multiple photocopies, you should not assume you have permission to publish an electronic copy online, even inside a VLE.

Web pages and images or other media found online have brought new challenges to copyright law. Many people believe that once something has been made available on the Web, it is in the public domain and thus free from copyright. This argument does not hold true because a book that has been published is also in the public domain. You can buy a copy; you can lend it; you can borrow it from the library; you might leave it on the bus; someone might give you it for nothing – but none of this means that the content is copyright free. It is true that authorship is often more difficult to ascertain with regard to web pages and it is also true that simple clicking, cutting and pasting make it easier to copy online materials. When students copy material from the Web and pass it off as their own, we call it plagiarism. When teachers do it in their work, it is considered illegal copying.

The most common temptations for teachers is to use images or diagrams that you find on the Web and put them into PowerPoint presentations or new web pages. A good rule-of-thumb is that if you do not own the image or know that it has been cleared for educational use, do not use it.

There are growing numbers of Web-based digital repositories, collections and databases of images, video, animation and audio that have been cleared and licensed for educational use – your university may also have its own collection. A good way to find digital collections in your subject area is via subject or discipline-specific gateways online, such as the Intute or through the web pages maintained by your university library.

FURTHER READING

Doyle, C. and Robson, K., *Accessible Curricula for All*. Cardiff: University of Wales Institute. Available at www.techdis.ac.uk/

Talbot, C., 2004. *Equality, Diversity and Inclusivity: Curriculum Matters*. SEDA Special Induction Pack 2. Birmingham: SEDA.

Waterfield, W. and West B., 2002. SENDA Compliance – An Audit and Guidance Tool for Accessible Practice within the Framework of Teaching and Learning. Southwest Academic Network for Disability Supports (SWANDS), University of Plymouth. Available at www.plymouth. ac.uk/assets/SWA/Sendadoc.pdf

 USEFUL WEB RESOURCES

British Dyslexia Association (BDA) www.bda-dyslexia.org.uk/

The BUFVC (British Universities Film and Video Council) promotes the production, study and use of film and related media in higher and further education and research. At the core of the BUFVC are its information services – a library and several online databases (www.bufvc.ac.uk/)

The Copyright Licensing Agency Ltd (CLA) provides information about copyright law (www.cla.co.uk/index.html)

Fleming, N., 2001. VARK: A Guide to Learning Styles. Lincoln University, New Zealand (www.vark-learn.com/English/index.asp)

JISC Legal Information Service provides information on various legal issues common to teachers in HE (www.jisclegal.ac.uk)

Quality Assurance Agency for Higher Education, 1999. Code of practice for the assurance of academic quality and standards in higher education, Section 3: Students with disabilities (www.qaa.ac.uk/academicinfrastructure/codeOf Practice/default.asp)

Intute provides subject gateways for finding good quality teaching resources online. Many have been cleared to educational use or include copyright information about their use (www.intute.ac.uk)

Intute Virtual Training Suite tutorials cover evaluating Web resources (www. vts.intute.ac.uk/)

The Technical Advisory Service for Images (TASI) is a service funded by the Joint Information Systems Committee (JISC), set up to advise and support the UK academic community on the digital creation, storage and delivery of image-related information (www.tasi.ac.uk/)

Chapter 8

Supporting your learners

INTRODUCTION

The increasing number and diversity of the student population means that teachers have less contact time with individuals, although they have a greater and wider variety of needs for support and guidance. In this chapter, ways of providing both face-to-face and virtual support in the context of academic and pastoral tutoring will be reviewed. The importance of the progress file and university services will be considered, as well as ways of developing autonomy in learners.

STUDENT SUPPORT IN THE CONTEXT OF WP/STUDENT DIVERSITY

The increase in student numbers in higher education in the UK, together with the WP agenda, have led to the creation of a larger and more diverse student population. In turn, the massive expansion of HE has generally led to a reduction in staff–student ratios and a change in the nature of the teaching, with an increased reliance on large group teaching methods at the expense of smaller group tutorial and seminar classes. These two factors are in direct opposition to each other in terms of providing support for students. The increasingly diverse nature of the students with more varied and potentially more demanding support requirements comes at a time when a reduction in staff–student contact time inhibits the ability of teaching staff to form a relationship with the students on their courses and hence their ability to respond directly to the needs of individual learners. This has implications for student support and retention.

Student recruitment and retention may be seen as two sides of the same coin and HEIs have a responsibility to ensure that all students accepted onto their courses have an equal opportunity to succeed. An increasing body of research on student retention (see in particular Yorke, 1999), has identified the most crucial time to support students, the time when they are most vulnerable. This is when making the transition to HE from school, or other prior study either in the UK or overseas, requiring adjustment to a different learning and teaching environment that may seem more aloof and uncaring, and which demands that students take a greater level of personal responsibility for their studies. Some students find it difficult to make this transition and are unable to cope with the academic demands placed on them. Induction and support during this transition is vital to ensure that all students are familiarised with academic expectations and are provided with early opportunities for formative feedback so that they develop in their learning ability and hence their confidence.

Widening participation initiatives aim to attract students from lower socio-economic backgrounds and from families with no prior experience of participation in HE. This can mean that students are unclear what to expect and in turn what is expected from them. This is also likely to be an area where their families cannot give them support directly. A key issue in student retention is for students to achieve social and academic integration early on – i.e. they need to have made friends and feel 'part of' the institution within the first few weeks of their course. Even nominally full-time students may have significant travel time to and from their place of study, or have outside commitments such as part-time work or caring responsibilities – all of which can impact on their ability to integrate and socialise with their student peer group and engage with informal support networks that contribute to their sense of 'belonging'. International students need time to adjust to their new surroundings and may experience culture shock and home-sickness. Students who study at a distance on online courses and do not attend regular face-to-face classes are likely to feel more isolated than traditional on-campus learners. The challenge for online tutors is to provide support that promotes contact between tutors and students, and between groups of students to keep learners engaged and motivated.

The diversity of students and the different routes by which they have entered higher education means that students come differently prepared for study at that level and we can no longer assume the knowledge and skills (particularly study skills) that they come equipped with.

150

To summarise, it is clear from this that support for students on a course is required to perform a number of different functions:

- to provide information to students about institutional processes and procedures;
- to provide information to students about academic expectations;
- to provide a mechanism for giving feedback as well as academic support and guidance to individual students;
- to provide personal welfare support to students and referral to other support agencies or information;
- to familiarise students with the culture of the institution and provide an opportunity for them to integrate with the institution and develop a sense of belonging;
- to help students in the development of their study and employability skills, and in their own personal and professional development.

SUPPORT AND COURSE DESIGN

In the context of course design, it is important to consider how learners on your course will be supported. As much as you may be willing, competing demands on your time make it impractical for you to make yourself available to students whenever they need you. As we have said already, the numbers of students involved and the range of issues they may present is likely to be too great for you to respond to all equitably, and this type of access is likely to be used regularly by some students and not at all by most. You therefore need to decide how you will structure and manage the way you support your learners to make the best use of the available time and resources that you and they have.

When and what support?

The Higher Education Funding Council for England (HEFCE) in their guidance on good practice in writing WP strategies (HEFCE, 2001) have broken down activities into phases, as shown in Table 8.1, which reflect the student life-cycle to indicate the types of support that are required.

In this chapter we will be concentrating on supporting students from their arrival, through the course to employment.

TABLE 8.1 Phases of student support

Phase	Type of activity
Aspiration raising	Demistifying HE, through marketing and recruitment activities such as HE taster days, open days, summer schools, mentoring, shadowing, school visits
Pre-entry activities	Helping students make the transition to a specific course, including WP activities run through strategic partnerships with schools and colleges
Admissions	Entry to course-admissions policies, procedures and monitoring, including consideration of the qualities and needs of part-time, postgraduate students and students with disabilities
First term/ semester	Starting a course: induction/orientation activities; range of learning and teaching strategies to support non-standard entry – e.g. diagnostic testing, study skills support, personal tutoring, PDPs
Moving through the course	Progressing through a course, including personal and academic tutoring, skills support, maths support, inclusive learning and teaching practices
Employment	Transition from course to work, embedding key skills within curricula, work-placement activities and careers guidance

Source: HEFCE, 2001.

Types of support

In general, there are two main types of support that students require:

1 **academic tutoring** – providing academic guidance to students to help them through their course of study;
2 **pastoral care** – helping students with personal problems that may impinge on their ability to study.

This can be offered in a range of ways and by the same or different types of staff. Models and examples of both types of support system are given in the next section.

MODELS OF SUPPORT

Earwaker (1992) outlines two overall strategies for providing student support. One is to provide a safety net for those students who have problems or who come into difficulties (which could be considered to be a remedial or curative approach). Another, preferred, strategy is to have a system of support that is part of the normal arrangements made for all students and which aims to enhance the student experience for the benefit of all (and is a preventative approach).

Two models that are commonly employed for providing student support are also discussed by Earwaker (1992):

- Pastoral care model: a traditional 'British' model of support offered via a personal tutoring system that is undertaken largely by untrained academic staff. Students are paired up with a personal tutor and some minimum level of expectation with regard to tutor availability is set out by the department or institution. It is a resource-intensive model that relies on academic staff making themselves readily available to students, or for a limited time only via an appointment system/office hours.

- Professional model: a referral model in which counselling is offered by trained, qualified professionals – e.g. in a central student support function that may be provided via the student union, counselling service or student welfare office. This type of support is readily available to students, but in effect deals with only one side of the story as it is independent of the student's department and does not feed back information to the tutor.

As neither of these two approaches, on its own, is an adequate model of student support, these two systems can and do exist side by side in many HEIs, and can be offered as either two separate or complementary approaches to supporting students. In this chapter we are concerned mostly with the types of department-based student support and how this can be achieved and enhanced.

Integrating support within the curriculum

Earwaker (1992) offers a third, preferred model of support:

- Integrated model: support is embedded within the curriculum so that all students routinely benefit from regular or timetabled contact with a tutor, irrespective of whether they are encountering difficulties.

In both of the examples below student support is delivered as part of and directly related to the course, rather than via an optional or ad hoc counselling role. However, even taking a structured approach, such as the incorporation of study skills modules, many tutors do not feel they possess the skills adequately enough themselves to be able to teach good practice to their students. In this case, the provision of study packs and questionnaires (see progress file questions) for both students and tutor provides a framework for the tutorials – whether they are delivered on an individual or group basis – and alleviates the tutor from some of the uncertainty and anxiety they may have about taking on the personal tutoring role. We will look at what the role of the personal tutor entails in the next sections, but first, we will flag another potential model for student support and that is for students to support each other (see p. 160).

EXAMPLE: STUDY SKILLS/TUTORIAL MODULE

A study skills module is used as a vehicle for academic and pastoral tutoring at level 1. Students in small groups (e.g. of up to 10) meet for a timetabled hour with their tutor on a weekly basis. A study pack is provided by the course leader for both students and tutors. Each week a different study/key/transferable skill is considered, for example:

- essay and/or report writing
- note-taking skills
- library skills – searching for, evaluating and referencing resources
- IT skills – wordprocessing, spreadsheets, presentation software
- time management
- team work
- revision techniques
- CV writing.

Through these tutorials students are taught what constitutes good practice in each of the skills. Students are then able to audit their own skills, identify their own development needs and are given the opportunity to practise and enhance their skills through either formative or summative assessment. These tutorials also serve as a vehicle for the pastoral tutoring system. Students are able to ask ongoing questions of their tutor about the course and other help that they need in a more informal setting.

Liverpool John Moores University

EXAMPLE: PROGRESS FILE REVIEW MEETINGS

Academic tutoring is delivered via the use of a progress file or portfolio in which students audit their own skills and reflect on their learning and development. Students are expected to answer a short questionnaire (see Figure 8.1) prior to meeting their tutor on an individual basis and this is then used as a discussion agenda for the meeting. This provides structure and focus for the meeting, enables students to identify their own development areas and their plans to address them. It aims to create an environment in which problems can be pre-empted and discussed in a routine manner. Meetings of this type would normally be held at least once per term or semester, and in particular after any assessment periods have ended so that progress can be reviewed. The example described involves students seeing their personal tutor three times per year – once at the start of the year and after the assessment period at the end of each of two semesters.

School of Geography, University of Leeds

WAYS OF SUPPORTING STUDENTS

As a new teacher in higher education it is unlikely that you will be able to influence the design of the system by which support is offered to individual learners. The key issues for you to consider are the extent to which the system of student support is either:

- **reactive** – e.g. you wait until a student comes to you with a problem and it is very much left to the student to identify that they have a problem and then (potentially having to overcome shyness or embarrassment) to take the initiative to arrange to see you;
- or **proactive** – e.g. you have a regular tutorial with individuals or groups of students to review their progress as a matter of course and not because they have any particular need, such that some potential problems may be pre-empted and discussed more generally;

155

Level 1, Semester 1, Meeting

Date and time of meeting with Personal Tutor: ....
Modules taken, Level 1, Semester 1:
Record any known marks so far:

Code Total Number	Name	Credits marks	Coursework mark	Exam marks

Examples of various types of work undertaken   (to highlight variety of skills practised – e.g. group posters on ..., written essay on...., individual presentation on ...., summary of .... etc. Be specific and give a variety):

Most enjoyable aspect of course and least enjoyable aspect of course and university life so far:

Outside activities (e.g. clubs joined, sports, voluntary work, part-time employment, leisure interests):

Any problems? (e.g. time management, module organisation, managing part-time work, accommodation hassles, other worries):

Things I have achieved so far that are important to me (e.g. can take better lecture notes, learnt to cook, understand ...., can find my way around campus):

Things I need to work hard on in future (e.g. be more careful with money, attend 9am lectures, get fit for fieldwork, read more textbooks):

Action plan for the next semester (e.g. I will .... by .... Plans for the summer vacation, applying for work experience and internships):

School of Geography, University of Leeds

FIGURE 8.1 Progress file review meeting questionnaire

and whether it is either:

- **integral** – e.g. you have formally timetabled contact time or that you come into regular teaching contact with individuals or groups of students;
- or **additional** to the programme or curriculum – e.g. tutors are expected to make their own arrangements with students as required.

Personal tutoring

Personal tutoring, whether delivered in groups via a tutorial/study skills module or on an individual basis, either informally or via timetabled or regular meetings, remains the departmental front-line support mechanism for students and may fulfil the functions of both academic and pastoral tutoring.

Personal tutors are generally academic staff who are allocated a number of students for whom they have a particular responsibility. The personal tutor role, particularly the pastoral care element, is one that many academic staff feel unqualified to undertake and which in many cases is ill-defined. Wheeler and Birtle (1993) suggest that there are various roles (some conflicting) the personal tutor can adopt, depending on their experience and comfort zone, or on the basis of what they think is expected of them:

- friend
- adviser
- referral agent
- academic assessor
- disciplinarian
- academic
- parent
- advocate
- counsellor
- teacher
- careers adviser
- referee
- confidant
- institutional change agent.

157

The wide-ranging and open-ended nature of the role has led some faculties or departments to allocate staff to undertake the role of tutoring specific groups of students – e.g. there may be a disability officer, international student support officer, year tutor – and/or staff may be given responsibility for advising students in specific areas – e.g. a placements tutor or departmental careers adviser. This enables staff to be trained and to develop expertise in specific areas of support so that they can advise students quickly and accurately. It also allows precise information to be given to students about who to go to for particular queries, so that students are not passed from one person to another before finding someone who can help them.

In some cases, the role of pastoral care is separated from the personal tutoring role, with support for personal matters being allocated to a single trained individual in a department. Students do not necessarily make the same distinctions between academic and personal problems as their teachers (and, indeed, problems themselves do not necessarily fall neatly into one of the two categories), so will often go to the personal tutor first, irrespective of the nature of the guidance they require. It is important, therefore, that in order to execute the role of 'referral agent' you need to be familiar with the support agencies that are available, both in the department and centrally at the university. In addition, you should understand the boundaries of your own role – i.e. to know where your job ends and someone else's begins. You should find out the range of student services available and keep a list of contact numbers to hand. This may be available from your department or institution – see the example on the next page.

In this era of litigation it is important that you do not advise students about issues that fall outside the remit of your job and about which you are not qualified to give advice. Although it may be difficult not to get embroiled in students' personal problems, you should establish ground rules, keep a professional distance, and you should not attempt to try to solve students' personal problems yourself.

As for acting the role of 'parent', the majority of learners in higher education will be 18 or over, which (in the UK) means they are above the legal age of responsibility, so tutors are not *in loco parentis*. Students should therefore take responsibility for their own decisions and actions, and you should not make contact with central support services on their behalf, but encourage them to do so for themselves.

EXAMPLE: STUDENT SUPPORT NETWORK

A network of central student services at the university produce a booklet outlining the range of support services that are available, what each service offers and how to get in touch with them. Copies of this booklet are given to all students and staff in a range of formats – e.g. bookmarks and leaflets. The network of student services also has a website providing equivalent information with a link from the student intranet site. The range of services includes:

- Accommodation Services
- Careers Centre
- Chaplaincy
- Equality Unit
- Graduate Training and Support Centre
- International Student Office
- Student Medical Practice
- Security Services
- Skills Centre
- Student Advice Centre
- Student Counselling Centre.

University of Leeds

Managing the role of personal tutor

In order to manage your own workload, you need to make it clear to your tutees how they can contact you, what your response time will be (e.g. you will respond to email enquiries within 24 hours or two working days etc.) and when you will be available outside any formal contact time that you have with them, for example:

- open door policy – where you are willing to see students at any time when you are in your office;
- surgery times – to indicate hours when you will be available to see students without an appointment (posted on your door or on a website);
- appointment system – indicating to students how quickly they will be able to arrange an appointment with you, or you could

publicise time slots on your door so that students can fill in their name against a particular slot to book an appointment with you;

■ online support – whether you will be regularly checking online discussion groups or will be available in a chat room.

In addition, it is important that you keep written records of all encounters with your personal tutees, by retaining a record of all email correspondence, or writing minutes of meetings. In all cases, you should briefly state the nature of the problem, together with a record of any discussion, the agreed actions to be taken and any follow-up required. A copy of these minutes should also be given to the student to remind them about who agreed to do what and by when.

Monitoring students' progress

We have talked so far about personal tutoring for supporting students across an entire programme of study and about the need to be both proactive and reactive with that support. One way that you can be proactive is by monitoring students' progress – e.g. through keeping attendance and assessment records. In some institutions, this may be achieved via the Student Information Management System (SIMS) and any successive periods of absence – e.g. missing two lectures – or a piece of assessed work that is not submitted may trigger an automatic letter to the student requiring them to meet with their personal tutor. In other cases, it may be necessary for the personal tutor to maintain and monitor these records themselves.

If your teaching responsibility is limited and you only have contact with students over part of a course, you should ensure that you keep a record of attendance for the time that you see them and monitor assignment submissions (both timeliness and quality), so that you are aware of any changes in an individual student's activity pattern and can be proactive in following the department's procedures for contacting anyone who appears to be going adrift.

Students supporting students – peer support

Students are a rich, but relatively untapped, resource for supporting their fellow students. Many universities are now introducing mentoring or 'buddying' schemes within their undergraduate curriculum. This involves students at higher levels of study supporting those who are at

---

EXAMPLE: PEER SUPPORT SYSTEMS

- Pairing final-year or second-year students with first years on the same degree programme.
- Postgraduate or final-year students delivering tutorial/study skills modules.
- Students at higher levels 'parenting' groups of incoming students.
- Home students being paired with overseas students.
- Students being helped to form their own support groups – e.g. mature or overseas students.
- Organising activities, including social, that involve participation by students in different years.

---

earlier stages in their studies and can be achieved either in a student-led or tutor-led manner.

The benefits of this type of support are that it may alleviate some of the pressures on teaching staff time, while providing good opportunities for students at higher levels to gain mentoring experience and to develop their communication skills. Learners may find their mentor or buddy more approachable and more readily available than teaching staff.

Clearly, this type of support system relies on students at higher levels of study being trained to undertake this supporting role and for sufficient numbers to be willing to help those less experienced than themselves. It may not be possible to run this system entirely on the basis of volunteers and it may be necessary to provide inducements for mentors – e.g. through payment or by formalising the role within the curriculum of the student mentors so that involvement in the scheme can lead to the award of academic credits. This latter approach may be contentious, but an example where this is used is given on the next page.

Using technology to support your students

The content and communication tools offered by Web technologies, personal digital assistants (pda) and mobile phones offer a range of ways in which you can support your students to ensure that they get the best learning experience. In the last ten years, the use of email to contact individual or groups of students has transformed the work of tutors and pastoral support roles. Email also makes it possible for you to respond

161

EXAMPLE: PROCTORING

Third-year students act as 'proctors' and meet with first-year students in tutor groups once a week for an hour. These are called 'proctorials' and in them the students discuss a piece of reading and associated questions that have been set by the lecturer that week. The students get a chance to discuss the set work and their views on the subject in an informal, non-threatening environment. This helps the students to gel as a group and to develop the skills needed for philosophical debate. The proctors receive training and their role involves chairing and facilitating the discussion, taking a register and liaising regularly with the tutor. This type of support forms part of the pastoral care arrangements and students are encouraged to ask their proctor general questions about student life. Through this activity the proctors themselves develop people management and communication skills. 'Proctoring' is available as a final-year module and proctors are required to submit a 1,500-word piece of written work for assessment, which brings together their training and experience through answering a series of fictitious scenarios.

George Macdonald-Ross, Department of Philosophy, University of Leeds

---

with feedback quickly to individuals or to a group without having to wait for the next class meeting time. Email, text and online discussion has revolutionised staff–student communication and made peer support and group discussion possible outside the time and space confines of the classroom. We no longer have to bump into students in corridors or catch them by phone when they are at home.

Structured support interventions such as proctoring can also make use of VLE discussion rooms. Online discussion rooms provide a way of posting messages to be viewed by a group. All the messages sent to a discussion room appear in one place and participants visit the discussion room to access them. Some staff choose to combine online communication modes using chat rooms, discussion rooms and email for support. With regard to using email and discussion tools for communication, Salmon (2000, p. 157) suggests that email should be used when you have 'a message for one or several people that you don't want everyone else to see or they don't need to see' and that group discussion or conferencing tools should be used when 'the message is intended for everyone in a particular group; you expect that everyone in the group will have the right to reply; there is benefit from everyone in the group seeing replies'.

Chat rooms particularly seem to encourage easy communication between students, often with a social slant, which may encourage them to provide informal peer support. By setting students specific tasks and reviewing their contributions in an online discussion room, you (or a proctor) can identify areas for extra support.

In the case of distance learning, if you have experience of being an online distance learner yourself, you may be able to remember the things that the teacher did that helped you to stay on course. If you have never been in that situation, it is worth finding out more about how to be an online tutor if this is part of your teaching responsibility.

SUPPORT FOR STUDY SKILLS DEVELOPMENT

As we said in the introduction to this chapter, the diversity of students and the different routes by which they have entered higher education mean that students come differently prepared for their studies. We cannot assume, therefore, that they come equipped with the study skills required to undertake their course. Some of the relevant skills are defined by the Qualifications and Curriculum Authority (QCA) (www.qca.org.uk) in the UK which, along with others, were defined in Table 6.11 on p. 124. Many of these skills are expected to be developed throughout a course and are also key or transferable skills that will benefit students once they graduate and enter the workplace, and so support employability. Perhaps the most important skill of all in this respect is the ability to improve one's own learning and performance as, through this, students develop an understanding of how they learn and are encouraged to take responsibility for and manage their own learning. This enables students to become more effective and independent learners, and better prepares them for life-long learning.

In the UK, skills of this nature are now articulated within benchmarking statements (see www.qaa.ac.uk) for different subjects and reflect the relative emphasis on the different skills within a subject context. In addition, there are skills that are specific to study at this level and which students may come with varying abilities in, such as:

- notetaking and summarising
- effective reading

- revision and exam techniques
- information literacy.

Until fairly recently, there was a general assumption and expectation by HE teachers that students came to university already proficient in study and key skills, but it is now recognised that this is not the case. These skills need to be taught, practised and made explicit in both learning outcomes and assessment (and especially in the marking criteria and feedback given) in order for them to be developed.

Auditing students' skills

From a course design perspective, it is necessary to decide on a strategy for supporting students to develop their study and key skills, but as part of this strategy the first question to ask is how will you and your students know what skills they already have? Ways of finding this out are through:

- diagnostic testing – e.g. of all students on entry to a course;
- student self-audit – e.g. through questionnaires or web-based skills development packages.

If you are going to explore strategies for diagnostic testing, don't forget to think about the various computer or web-based tools that may be available. We discussed the use of computers in assessment in Chapter 6 and many teachers use computer-based test tools to set up quizzes that students can do early in a module to diagnose gaps in their knowledge or skills. Some of the computer-based testing software has functionality to point students to specific resources, depending on the marks they achieve or the answers they have given. This adaptive testing can be used to make model answers available and to suggest paths for further research or to background knowledge. Many of these tools can be set either to send a report (by an individual) to the teacher or to show results to the students. It may be that you can use a similar tool to diagnose and then target the support you are offering to those in the most need.

Approaches to supporting students' skills development

One can also take a reactive or proactive approach and provide training in skills either as additional or integral to the core curriculum. A reactive

---

EXAMPLE: DIAGNOSTIC TESTING FOR MATHEMATICS

MATHLETICS is a computer-based test for mathematical skills that is used for diagnosis and continual assessment of engineering, mathematics and biological sciences students at Brunel University. The outcomes of the test are fed back to the tutor to form the basis of discussions and advice to the students and also to give an overview of the class skills, which informs the level 1 lecturers and admissions tutors.

Other case studies of how universities in the UK have used diagnostic testing for mathematics can be found at http://mathstore.ac.uk/mathsteam/ together with further information about the range of support that is available for students to develop their mathematical skills.

---

approach is to provide a safety-net for students by referring those who demonstrate, or are (self-)diagnosed as having insufficient skill in an area to a central support unit or skills centre. As we said earlier, this approach on its own is inadequate and certainly the skills unit would be likely to buckle under the pressure of student numbers if this were the sole source of support. In addition, this service may not attract those who are most in need of support, but rather those who are most conscientious or anxious about their skills – e.g. mature learners – and the general good practice that is taught may be difficult for them to translate to the subject-context and specific expectations of their course.

Another reactive approach is to direct students towards skills training manuals or web-based packages, but again, without embedding the use of such packages within the curriculum, they are unlikely to be used by any but the keenest students. Although your students may be confident users of web-based materials and computer packages, there is always a learning curve for any user when faced with a new package, and online assessment tools or VLEs are no exception. The specific package that is used on your campus may not have the same features or navigation as environments your students have used before. What is important is that students spend their time on task, not struggling with technical issues (Littlejohn and Higgison, 2003), so you should support your students by ensuring they have access to handbooks, guides and technical support, perhaps by phone as well as in computer clusters for any package you are using in your teaching.

Embedding support for students' skills development within the curriculum

Approaches that are proactive and integrate study skills training within the curriculum are:

- Study skills or tutorial module
  - Study skills delivered by academic staff or postgraduates as part of a credit-bearing module that may also act as a vehicle for personal tutoring.
  - Students may see these types of modules as less significant than their subject content unless they are placed within the subject context – examples where this is achieved are given on the next page.

- Integrate skills development within existing modules
  - As an alternative to a separate skills-based module, skills can be embedded within existing modules at all levels by making them explicit in both the learning outcomes and assessment criteria. This aims to ensure that relevant skills are practised and assessed as part of all modules and can be developed by the student based on appropriate feedback.
  - This approach requires careful mapping of skills and staging of their delivery across the entire programme. This may be achieved through writing a Programme Specification, as discussed in Chapter 2.

- Teaching skills in tutorials in existing modules
  - It may be possible for you to dedicate, in a timely manner, specific tutorial sessions within your own modules for the delivery of study skills.
  - You could deliver a session on essay/report writing a couple of weeks before an assignment is due, or a session on revision techniques in the week before the end of term. This will help to ensure that students are familiar with the course conventions and expectations.

EXAMPLE: INTRODUCTION TO HISTORICAL SKILLS

As part of a core first-year module, students read closely one or two pieces of historical writing. Through this students learn to read critically, use the English language correctly, develop good practice in the compilation of bibliographies and footnotes, develop effective approaches to studying and learning, make oral presentations, and design and write essays.

Simon Burrows, School of History, University of Leeds

EXAMPLE: PRACTICAL SKILLS IN CHEMISTRY

Through this first-year module, students learn to work safely in a chemical laboratory, keep appropriate records of laboratory work and write laboratory reports in an appropriate style, record data and physical measurements, and comment on their precision and accuracy, prepare simple organic and inorganic compounds, and use selected chemical apparatus and instruments in the appropriate manner.

Terry Gibb, School of Chemistry, University of Leeds

Supporting study skills via the Web

The use of a VLE to support the management of your course is discussed in detail in the following chapter, but it is worth considering how putting your materials for a module into the VLE can help with study support. By collecting study materials, handouts and readings together in the VLE, you are providing a visual map of the work that has to be covered and some kind of navigation structure through it. This can be very useful to students when they start to struggle with workloads. Some teachers choose to 'time release' materials in the VLE, while others put up support materials for each lecture at the start of the module. This allows students to look forward to materials later in the module and relate their immediate learning to what will be coming. There are also examples of modules in which teachers have used the VLE to provide self-assessment style tests after lectures to allow students to assess their own comprehension of the

167

topics covered. User tracking tools have shown that students engage with these regularly across the course of the module and return to them in anticipation of the exam.

PROGRESS FILES

Progress files are a relatively recent introduction into UK higher education, originally following a recommendation by Dearing (1997). A progress file is a record of achievement that consists of two elements:

1   A transcript that is provided by the insitution to students at each stage of their study and which records their achievement in different elements of the course (rather than just the overall grade).
2   A means by which students can monitor, build and reflect on their personal development.

In this section, we are mostly concerned with the latter part, which is owned by the student and is aimed at developing an individual's ability to reflect on their own learning and achievement, and plan for their own personal educational and career development – referred to as personal development planning (PDP). This is an important process through which students can develop the skills and attitudes required for independent and life-long learning.

In the context of student diversity, Brennan (2004) suggests that the provision of a greater amount of relevant information about each graduate (i.e. about who they are, what they know and what they can do), which is recorded within their progress file, would 'lessen the attention given to non-relevant information such as their age, their social class, their gender or their ethnicity'. The transcript and PDP that form the progress file could therefore have a significant impact on the employability of graduates by providing them with confidence through knowing and being able to articulate their own skills and strengths.

There are many types of PDP tool in use – such as learning logs, diaries or portfolios – in both paper-based and web-based forms. In order to be successful, Personal Development Planning needs to be a mainstreamed activity that is structured and supported, and one that encourages students to bring together and reflect on both their academic and non-academic learning experiences – e.g. to include work experience and extra-curricular activities. It is also a process that enables tutors to monitor student progress, and can form the basis for discussion and the provision of academic support and guidance. Through the progress file, the aims and learning outcomes of the programme can be made explicit to students so that they can reflect on their performance in direct relation to what is to be achieved. For students to engage with the PDP process, they need to see that it is valued by the staff that support them and that it is valued by society – e.g. employers and professional bodies. Students are more likely to engage with and value the process if they see that academic staff themselves are involved in PDP processes – e.g. through appraisal or portfolio building linked to professional accreditation and continuing professional development requirements.

E-portfolios

The development of e-portfolios to support personal development planning is an initiative that is being supported at a national level in many countries. In the UK, personalised learning, electronic portfolios and personal development planning are key themes of the Government's e-strategy (DfES, 2005). Across years of study or employment, an individual will collect together evidence of their skills and achievements in their own dedicated online space. The difficult issues of security, portability and ownership continue to challenge those working on these new technology initiatives, but if these can be resolved, it is likely that you will be working with students who are developing their portfolio online, or at least, electronically.

EXAMPLES: ELECTRONIC PROGRESS FILES AND E-PORTFOLIOS

Centre for International E-Portfolio Development, University of Nottingham: www.nottingham.ac.uk/eportfolio/ePortfolios.html

LUSID: Personal Development Planning Support Tool, University of Liverpool: http://lusid.liv.ac.uk/index.html

The RAPID Personal Development Planning Tool, Construction and Civil Engineering, Loughborough University: http://rapid.lboro.ac.uk/

FURTHER READING

Bochner D., Gibbs, G. and Wisker, G., 1995. *Supporting More Students*. Teaching More Students Series, Oxford: Oxford Centre for Staff Development.

Earwaker, J., 1992. *Helping and Supporting Students: Rethinking the Issues.* Buckingham: Society for Research into Higher Education and Open University Press.

Mason O'Connor, K. and Oates, L., 1999. *Academic Tutoring.* SEDA Special No. 11. Birmingham: SEDA.

Wheeler, S. and Birtle, J., 1993. *A Handbook for Personal Tutors.* Buckingham: Society for Research into Higher Education and Open University Press.

Yorke, M., 1999. *Leaving Early: Undergraduate Non-completion in Higher Education.* London, Falmer.

 USEFUL WEB RESOURCES

Mathcentre: www.mathcentre.ac.uk/

Maths Stats and OR HE Academy Subject Network: www.mathstore.ac.uk/

Chapter 9

Managing your course

INTRODUCTION

In this chapter we look at how you can manage your course, course materials and students. There are several different roles and levels of management that exist in delivering a course, and this chapter will provide you with an opportunity to consider your own role and responsibilities within the course delivery team. We will consider factors that will help you to provide information and guidance about the outcomes, content and expectations of the course in a timely and effective manner. The place of the VLE as a course management tool and using the Internet as a teaching/learning resource are also key parts of this chapter.

COURSE MANAGEMENT

Course management has a dual role – for the purposes of quality assurance (assuring that procedures are followed and that outcomes and standards are met), together with guiding, informing and supporting the students and their learning. Several roles and levels of responsibility are involved in managing the delivery of a course and the students enrolled on it. These roles may be given a variety of names in your own institution:

- programme/course manager or leader
- module manager or leader
- academic tutor
- personal tutor
- pastoral tutor.

Some of these roles may be performed by the same person – e.g. you may find that the personal tutor performs both academic and pastoral tutoring roles (as was discussed in Chapter 8), or that the module leader role and that of the academic tutor are one and the same, with a separate personal (pastoral) tutor being allocated. Whether this is the case or not, it is unlikely that all the roles will be performed by a single person and it is also unlikely that you will have complete autonomy over the part of the course you are responsible for designing and delivering. It is clear, then, that the individuals given these differing roles and responsibilities need to be communicating with each other about many different aspects of the course:

- to discuss design and delivery of the overall course;
- to plan timetabling and resolve any issues (e.g. clashes);
- to liaise about the content and delivery of individual modules;
- to moderate assessments and their marking;
- to confer about individual students and their progress;
- and certainly about, and **before**, any changes are made to any aspect of the course.

You may find that discussions of this nature are formalised within departmental processes, such as the requirement to hold meetings to discuss any planned programme changes – e.g. learning and teaching committees or programme team meetings – and assessments – e.g. moderation meetings or examination boards. There are also other more informal opportunities for you to liaise with members of the course team and you should try to take advantage of discussions with experienced staff as a way of checking on, and generating ideas for, your own practice. You may find that you are allocated a mentor with whom you can discuss your teaching role and responsibilities. We will discuss this and other forms of peer evaluation in Chapter 10.

Your role in course management

In order to be effective in any one of the above roles you will need to be familiar with the definitions, policies, procedures and structures that operate at the institution where you work. Many of these will be specific to your institution or even local to your school or department, and it is your responsibility to find these out. Unfortunately, the response 'but I was never told the procedure' is unlikely to be a strong one in defending against a student appeals claim. The overall course leader would be a good first port of call to ask for advice and you should not feel that this will be seen as a sign of weakness or inability. You should also give feedback on any problems that arise and ask about any situations that you are unsure how to deal with.

Although you may not be called an 'academic tutor', it is most likely that students taking the course on which you teach will come to you for help and advice about some aspect of their study or outside life. You therefore need to be clear about your own role and the boundaries of it as outlined in Table 9.1.

COURSE DOCUMENTATION

Course documentation needs to be fit for purpose, so when developing and designing your part of the course you need to consider what information you will need to provide to students and how best you can provide it. Course documentation is a key source of information for students and can be an important factor in alleviating students' anxieties and uncertainties about their course. Table 9.2 outlines the range of course documentation.

The list shows that course documentation can serve a number of purposes. You need to decide what the purpose of each document is and who it is written for before you decide how/what to write in it and how to use it. For example, the module proforma and module handbook both provide a summary of the aims, outcomes, content and assessment of a module. However, a proforma is written for the purpose of module approval and is not aimed at students, so it may not be particularly user-friendly or reassuring for students on the module, and may provide insufficient information to form a basis for students to make decisions about whether to take a particular module or not.

In their most comprehensive form, module handbooks could contain all the session handouts, assessment briefings and reading lists for the whole module, but you may wish to consider the value of supplying big bulky documents to new students and whether you are actually informing students or just giving them a lot of paper all at once. You may also find that student attendance is poor if all the teaching materials are given in this form and the reason for doing so is not made clear to students. The timely release of information in smaller, more manageable chunks may mean that students are more likely to read and digest the contents, and this may turn out to be a more effective approach. You therefore need

173

TABLE 9.1 Roles and responsibilities

To ascertain your role and responsibilities, you should seek out answers to the following questions:

- What is my role?
  - Is the role defined anywhere – e.g. in a staff or student handbook?
  - Are there student expectations or entitlements set out anywhere – e.g. a Student Charter or partnership agreement?

- Are there particular roles assigned to other staff in the department?
  - For example, personal tutor, year tutor, placement tutor, disability officer?
  - If so, who are they and how (and when) should they be contacted?

- What are the institutional or departmental policies and procedures? Are there codes of practice for:
  - Academic and pastoral tutoring?
  - Assessment?
  - Attendance monitoring?
  - Record keeping?
  - Project supervision?

- What support structures are available across the institution?
  - For example, skills development, careers guidance, dyslexia support, language support?
  - If so, how (and when) should they be contacted?

- How will my undertaking of the role be evaluated and reviewed?
  - There may be formal mechanisms for this, such as student questionnaires and staff appraisal.

- Are there any staff development opportunities available to help me with my course management or tutoring role?

Source: Adapted from Mason O'Connor and Oates (1999).

to plan your strategy for providing information and guidance when designing the module.

Making course documentation available via a VLE

A relatively recent development in course management is the VLE. Most higher education institutions now have campus-wide or widely used

TABLE 9.2 Course documentation

Purpose	Document type	Possible contents
Course validation and Quality Assurance	Course validation document	Documentation prepared for course approval
	Programme specification	Map showing how overall course outcomes are achieved by the outcomes in individual modules
	Module proforma	A document prepared for module approval giving details of e.g. aims and learning outcomes, syllabus, assessment and readings lists
Orientation	Information about the institution	Policies and procedures at an institutional level, plus information about the social and support services the institution offers
	Departmental student handbook	Information about departmental policies, procedures, staff, facilities
Induction	Programme handbook	A document aimed at students on the course giving full details of the programme
	Module publicity materials	To enable students to make informed module choices from options
In-course information	Module handbooks	Documentation aimed at students on the module, giving details of the aims and learning outcomes, syllabus, assessment and reading lists
	Assessment briefings	Detailed information about the assessments in a module, the learning outcomes they aim to assess, the criteria against which work is assessed, hand-in dates and procedures, etc.
	Session outlines and handouts	Discussed in Chapter 7
	Reading lists	Indicating relevant resources, preferably annotated.

VLEs. In the USA, these are often referred to as Learning Management Systems (LMS). VLEs are web-based environments designed specifically to provide easy access for teachers and tutors to online tools that will enable you to support and manage learning on your course in new and scalable ways.

JISC, the Joint Information Systems Committee in the UK, offer the following definition of a virtual learning environment:

> A Virtual Learning Environment is a collection of integrated tools enabling the management of online learning, providing a delivery mechanism, student tracking, assessment and access to resources. These integrated tools may be one product (e.g. BlackBoard, WebCT) or an integrated set of individual, perhaps open-source, tools.
>
> (www.jiscinfonet.ac.uk)

The tools available to you to assist in organising your online materials vary. You can usually upload either single documents or create folders to group materials by week, group or topic. It is worth setting aside some time to think about, or get advice on, how to organise your materials so that it doesn't become chaotic as the course progresses. Some teachers choose to upload all their course materials into the VLE at the start of the course, while others add new materials each week as the students progress. If you are teaching as part of a team, check what your colleagues are doing so that students are clear about what kind of materials will be published and when they can expect them to appear in the VLE. If you are the main tutor for your course, you may be able to use the VLE to control access to specific resources or activities in the VLE. Some teachers use the time-release methods to give questions on one day and then answers the next or set specific times (a number of days) for participation in a group discussion online. Putting materials online enables you to make learning materials available to your students 'any time, any place, any pace' as long as they have access to the Web.

Some people argue that provision of online materials is just about shifting cost – making students print off materials individually instead of using departmental photocopy budgets. If you are concerned about this shift in costs, there is nothing to stop you giving paper handouts in class. There are, however, specific benefits that can be gained by also publishing online materials.

TIMING AND QUANTITY OF INFORMATION

Work by the Open University (Tresman, 2002) has shown that the timing and quantity of information provided to students can have an impact on student retention. In particular, some of the factors that can increase students' tendencies to withdraw are:

- an overload of complicated information;
- a confusing array of points of contacts and information;
- conflicting information;
- a lack of information;
- mismatch between expectations and the realities of the course of study.

It is evident from this that clear, accurate, consistent information in well-structured documentation is important, and that the quantity of information provided and the timing of its distribution needs to be carefully planned. Tresman (2002) advises that you should provide information, advice and guidance in a range of formats – electronic, paper-based, verbal, on notice-boards, etc. – and that, whether for current or prospective students, it should reflect accurately the focus and content of the course, and make expectations clear by painting a real-istic picture of the time commitment (both contact time and private study), workload and level of difficulty involved. You will also need to ensure that your module information is in agreement with that in the overall programme handbook, even if these are written by different people.

Similarly, Yorke (1999) has undertaken considerable research in the area of student retention and suggests that there are three major reasons for non-completion, namely:

- wrong choice of programme;
- financial difficulties;
- quality of student experience.

The provision of accurate and realistic information about a course, together with the timing and manner in which it is provided can have an impact on two of the above three factors.

Other factors that can contribute to students staying on a course are early contact and on-going dialogue with their tutor, together with prompt and encouraging feedback. Equally important, though, are social and academic integration. Part of managing a course is to generate a sense of cohort for those who are studying together, to provide oppor-tunities for students to mix with both staff and each other, and to facilitate students working together so that they can form friendships and provide peer support for each other.

COURSE INDUCTION

Course induction is a key part of managing a course and there is often an 'induction week' at the start of the academic year to welcome new and returning students. In the case of first-year students, induction provides a vital opportunity for students to form friendships in the first weeks while helping them to develop the study and survival skills they will need for the course and so provide them with a firm foundation for their study (see examples in Table 9.3). The induction process can be spread throughout the first term or semester to avoid overload of information at the start. For returning students, induction introduces them to their next year's study and provides an opportunity to choose options and enrol on modules if this has not been done in the previous academic year.

COURSE HANDBOOKS

Course documentation, whether at an institutional, school, programme or module level, plays a vital part in introducing students to their programme of study and the standards and expectations of the higher education system they are entering.

As we have said already, before you start writing a course handbook you need to be clear about its purpose and who it is aimed at. You will also need to liaise with the overall course leader about the content to ensure that you do not contradict or duplicate unnecessarily any information that is produced elsewhere. What you do need to provide is all the essential information that students need to enable them to pursue their studies and even to pre-empt some of the questions they may wish to ask. A comprehensive list of possible contents is given in Table 9.4. You would need to select the sections that are relevant to your own teaching context.

COURSE MANAGEMENT USING TECHNOLOGY

Developments in interoperability between large systems and software means that increasingly VLEs are being integrated to work in conjunction with other campus systems such as the student records system, campus email, library catalogue, plagiarism detection service, student tracking, personal development portfolios and module evaluation tools. In some places, portals are being created that provide students and staff

▓ TABLE 9.3 Induction weeks

EXAMPLES

At Sheffield Hallam University the Admissions Department send out welcome letters and pre-arrival information, tailored to each course, to all new students. The Students' Union put together a week of activities, and the Student Services Centre offers various support to staff and students over the induction period plus throughout the year. Each faculty has its own way of organising the induction period for new students, but in general the induction aims to achieve the following:

● Orientation

Students are introduced to the university and their accommodation:

- they get to find their way around both the geographical layout and the structural organisation of the university

- large signs and student helpers are used.

● Social

Students are welcomed by their department and course:

- they get to meet both teaching and support staff, their fellow students, plus students in other years of the course

● Support services

Students are introduced to the university's support infrastructure:

- they receive induction to learning resource centres, student union, student services centre, computing facilities and meet their course representative.

● Academic

Students are introduced to their course and the academic expectations:

- they are given handbooks, timetables, book lists

- expectations about study skills are clarified and they are introduced to learning styles

- they receive guidance about assessment regulations, options and progression routes.

● Administrative

Students are registered on their course and enrolled on modules:

- they sort out their student card and Student Union membership.

Some time is built in to the week for students to meet others, to browse and explore their new surroundings and to reflect on their new experiences.

Nottingham University sends out a pack to 28,000 students that has a timetable of week one events and also a checklist of things to remember when coming to university. They have a dedicated website for their 'Freshers Week' (www.weekone.co.uk) that provides information for new students about the university, halls accommodation and the city. It gives guidance about what to bring, how to organise student finances and some general advice, and introduces them to the student life of parties and take-away pizzas.

■ TABLE 9.4 Contents of a course handbook

EXAMPLE

- Contents page/index
- Course aims and outcomes
- Introduction and rationale
- Course structure
- Details of any professional body accreditation
- Academic calendar – term dates and dates for submission of work
- Timetable – although this may be individual to a person rather than a course
- Range of modules – core, optional and elective
- Possible routes through the course (in both text and diagrams)
- Explanation of credits and progression criteria
- Descriptions of modules
- Module assessment methods and criteria
- Teaching staff – their availability and contact details
- Details of VLE plus use and availability of other C&IT
- Details of library and IT facilities – access and opening times
- Reading lists
- Expectations regarding private study time
- Guidelines regarding plagiarism and its avoidance
- Frequently Asked Questions and their answers or reference to page numbers where answers can be found
- Possible career options linked to pathways through the course
- Details of disability support services and any English language support available
- Health & Safety regulations (if applicable)

Source: School of Engineering, Liverpool John Moores University

with access to all the information and tools they need to manage their courses and resources online. Even if you do not feel that you want to design an online course or make your learning materials available online, it is worth finding out whether you can use the integrated systems for emailing to class groups, online reading lists, gathering marks and module evaluation. If you are teaching as part of a team, there may be time-saving benefits (as well as more seamless experience for your students) to getting everyone in the team to use the same VLE tools.

VLEs and LMS have been designed to allow different levels of permissions to different users. Commonly, there are global access permissions to change and move materials granted to only a few users. The responsibility for maintaining specific course or module areas is then devolved to the course leader and further to teachers and tutors. In order to use any VLE on campus, you will need a password and appropriate permissions. The support team or helpdesk who give you your password will be able to explain the various access level permissions you have been given. If you are not the course leader, you may not have permission to structure the course space online, but as a tutor, unless you are teaching from other people's pre-written materials, you should have permission to upload documents and make use of communication tools for discussion and feedback.

Some VLEs include specific timetable or calendar tools into which you can enter events on your course, such as lecture or lab time and submission deadlines for assessment. These can then be seen by all your students when they log in. If your VLE does not have this functionality, you may still want to think about having a timetable included in your web-based resources for the course. This has the advantage of being easily updatable by you if the timetable changes. If you do this, ensure that the students understand that the timetable on the Web is the one that will be updated and that they should check it for changes. You may be able to use tracking functionality in the VLE to see which of your students has read particular pieces of information and this can help you to know whether information about timetable changes is getting through.

STUDENT DIVERSITY AND COURSE MANAGEMENT

As we discussed in Chapter 7, it cannot be assumed that students are familiar with the nature of higher education and what is expected, so course documentation needs to ensure that standards and expectations are made explicit. You also need to ensure that any documentation and associated reading lists do not assume a gender, ethnicity or cultural perspective, and that course documentation conforms to the guidelines for accessibility given in Chapter 7. To be accessible, course documentation – e.g. course handbooks, summaries, handouts, bibliographies, key readings, etc. – should be made available in advance of teaching sessions and in a range of formats so that students have more time to read and assimilate the information, and can prepare for sessions in advance so that they are able to come armed with questions and can take a more active part in the session. Be careful to ensure that your students know where in the VLE you have put them and that they have appropriate password/

TABLE 9.5 Ways of using a VLE

Uploading your handout materials and PowerPoint slides

- Even if you give these out in class, putting them into the VLE will ensure that any of your students who lose their copies will be able to find and print off others.
- Some of your students may prefer to have your materials in electronic formats so that they can store or annotate them on their own computer.
- If you would like your students to read through materials before coming to your class, publishing them into the VLE and letting your students know they will be there, is one way to distribute material without having to gather all your students together.

Producing 'hybrid' reading lists

- If you find that you are including resources on your reading list that are websites, e-books or articles in e-journals, the most direct way to help your students to access them may be to produce a page of links that, rather than being printed off, provides one click access to the resources.
- If your 'reading list' includes some audio, video or animation, the VLE can be used to link to or deliver these, allowing students to watch or listen in their own time and at their own pace.

Using communication tools to make announcements

- If your module or course has its own space in the VLE, there are probably tools that you can use to send emails to all the students on the course, or web-based bulletin boards for making announcements.
- Web-based bulletin boards are very useful for making announcements because they can be updated almost instantly, so you can ensure that the correct and most up-to-date information is getting to your students.

Publishing your own web-based teaching materials

- Many teachers now design and use their own web pages to describe or illustrate content for their course.

permissions to access them. You may want to develop a handout or handbook that explains about the resources you have made available online and how they should be used as part of the course.

If, when you were studying, someone had said to you 'I want you to attend a full timetable of lectures, understand all the content, contribute to group seminars, ask questions of your tutor, do library-based research, engage in group projects, evidence your learning, be independent, have a social life, have a part-time job, manage your family commitments and be active in student representation, *and* I would like you to log on and contribute to online discussions outside class time, even though it doesn't

TABLE 9.5 (continued)

- Some teachers develop 'online lectures'. This may involve bringing together text, images, animation and video into topic themes. In some cases, online lectures are used to replace, or substitute, face-to-face teaching. In other cases, the online lectures feed into group discussion or activities in class.

Using communication tools for many-to-many discussions online

- In Chapter 5 we discussed choosing appropriate learning activities for your group. One of the options open to you when using a VLE is to make use of the communication tools included in it. These are usually either synchronous chat tools or asynchronous discussion tools, or both.

- Chat tools and discussion tools can be used, with some forward planning, for seminar discussions, group work, debates, role play and question-and-answer formats. They have the advantage of offering you opportunities to change the pace and place of discussions you are having with your student group. They can also make it possible to monitor the progress of student groups or to get students who cannot meet together, working together.

Using quiz or test tools for formative assessment and feedback

- To aid learning, it is important for students to get regular opportunities to check their own understanding or test their skills. Most VLEs include some kind of online testing tool, usually offering a range of question types. Many teachers compile tests or quizzes on certain subjects and topic areas, and make them available to students to use as self-assessment or continuous assessment tools. Depending on the functionality available, it may be possible for you to decide that you want to track student progress in this way.

- All the quiz tools available include opportunities for teachers to attach feedback to particular answers or results. This can be a useful way to direct students to revision materials or further resources, or to explain common mistakes.

---

contribute to your marks', would you? Probably not – something would get dropped off your priorities. If you are making use of a VLE to support your teaching, think about how you can use it to help students reach their learning priorities.

You may choose to use the VLE in a variety of ways. In Chapter 7 we looked specifically at using handouts and audio-visual aids for a diverse group of students. Using a VLE helps you to be flexible in the ways and times you make materials available (see Table 9.5).

The growth in the use of VLEs in teaching has coincided with moves in university libraries to make more of their collection available online either through digitisation initiatives or subscription to online journals and databases. This technology is revolutionising the way we search for and find information. Books and journals that traditionally have been available in print form and are available to only one library user at a time can now be viewed by multiple users simultaneously, and materials from research collections that have been digitised can be used by students and teachers across the globe. It is unlikely that in any reading list you compile now you would not want to make use of some digital or web-based resources. 'Hybrid' reading lists are becoming increasingly common and using electronic formats for these lists enable you to create links for your students that can lead them directly to journal articles or other resources and library holdings. Some university libraries also have projects to develop online reading lists for specific modules. Librarians and subject specialist teams in the library are useful sources of information about initiatives and projects that are relevant to your teaching.

Since most students prepare their assignments in electronic formats, it makes sense in many courses to receive work electronically too. Some departments have experimented with the use of email or electronic pigeon holes for submitting work. Anecdotal feedback from students indicates that many appreciate the additional security and flexibility of this method over having to hand work in personally to a departmental office. Work received electronically has the added advantages of allowing students to submit work in a variety of formats or collect work in an online portfolio. If you are part of a teaching team where double marking is carried out, receiving work electronically can also enable two people to mark the work simultaneously without the need for additional photo-copying.

The use of electronic and online plagiarism detection tools is becoming more widespread in higher education in the UK. The tools search content for text matches in a specific set of documents or on the Web and present these to the marker for consideration. If you receive work in electronic formats you can make use of such tools if your university subscribes to them. Some teachers ask their students to run their own work through plagiarism checkers before submission (see p. 118), or to use this task as the basis for a discussion about plagiarism.

VLEs for distance delivery

Online courses, or 'purely online courses', are a very different undertaking from those using a VLE for on-campus teaching. Whereas on-campus teaching may make use of web-based tools for some part of the course delivery, where departments are developing courses for distance delivery VLEs are often used as the primary mechanism for providing access to content, communication, assessment and administration tools. With no face-to-face contact with students, many of the assumptions we make about how we know what our students are learning are challenged. If you find that you have responsibility for teaching or supporting groups of students who study at a distance, it is worth reading more about distance learning online and the specific skills you will need as a tutor. Salmon (2000, 2002) and Duggleby (2001) both describe in step-by-step detail how tutors on distance learning online courses can best support student learning.

 ## FURTHER READING

Frame, P., 2001. *Student Induction in Practice*. SEDA Paper No. 113, Birmingham: SEDA.

Mason O'Connor, K. and Oates, L. 1999. *Academic Tutoring*. SEDA Special No. 11. Birmingham: SEDA.

 ## USEFUL WEB RESOURCES

JISC Infonet – Effective Use of VLEs: www.jiscinfonet.ac.uk/

JISC Plagiarism Detection Service: www.submit.ac.uk/

Chapter 10

Does the course work?

INTRODUCTION

How do we measure the effectiveness of our teaching and student learning? This chapter looks at the process of evaluation and review, and identifies a range of strategies that can be used for gaining feedback on your course and on your own teaching. This will ensure that the planned learning outcomes and standards are met, and provide information that will allow you to develop the design and delivery of the course for the future.

EVALUATION AND COURSE DESIGN

As a new teacher in higher education, your experience of evaluating teaching and courses is likely to be the end-of-module questionnaire, when students are asked to provide their perceptions on the adequacy of the resources, standards of teaching and, perhaps, their overall satisfaction with the provision. To some, this type of questionnaire is seen as the evaluation process itself rather than as an information-gathering exercise, and is sometimes considered merely to be a **happy sheet**, giving a fairly superficial view of students' 'happiness' about their course immediately after it has ended. In some instances, this view has been consolidated and supported by the pressure for an on-going quality assurance process, which has meant that measuring the measurable has taken precedence over measuring quality.

In addition, such forms can include graded scales, enabling quantification, so that the results can be used as quality markers – an average score of 4 out of 5 (with 5 being the top) suggesting that all is well. While this process does provide some useful data, the results need to be treated with some caution: they only represent the views of a proportion of students, at a particular stage of the course (often directly before assessment), based on a selected range of stimulus questions. In addition, students are being asked for feedback on a number of their courses at the same time and, even if the questionnaires are online and automatically submitted, this can result in questionnaire fatigue. As a consequence, this method on its own is insufficient and lacking in rigour.

What we advocate here is that evaluation and review needs to be a more thoughtful process. This does not mean that it needs to take more time or that it adds to the administrative burden; rather that the process is comprehensive and fit for purpose. In the context of course design, the way in which the course is to be evaluated needs to be considered at the start and designed into a course from the outset.

PURPOSES OF EVALUATION

Evaluation may be defined as an objective process in which data is collected, collated and analysed to produce information or judgements on which decisions for action to improve practice may be based. Evaluation can operate at a range of levels and for a number of purposes. At the fundamental level of the individual lecturer and their own teaching, evaluation aims to enable teachers to:

- learn about the effects and effectiveness of their teaching;
- enhance the quality of their teaching;
- develop as teaching professionals.

Whereas at the level of the course, evaluation aims to:

- fulfil the institution's internal quality assurance requirements;
- determine whether the course aims and outcomes have been achieved;
- review whether the outcomes and their associated teaching learning and assessment strategies are appropriate;
- identify areas of the course that can be improved.

Evaluation can also be conducted at a subject or institutional level by external agencies such as, in the UK, the QAA. The outcomes of such evaluations can often be found in the form of league tables and can be used to inform interested parties – e.g. prospective students, their parents, employers, etc. – about the quality of the institution and its provision.

EVALUATION TERMINOLOGY

It may be apparent already that much of the terminology associated with evaluation is also common to that of assessment and many of the considerations about the purposes of assessment that were discussed in Chapter 6 are relevant here also. To continue in this vein, evaluation can be considered to be of two main types:

1   **Formative evaluation** – which, just as formative assessment, allows improvements to be made by identifying scope and potential for change and development.
2   **Summative evaluation** – which, just as in summative assessment, allows conclusions to be drawn that can form the basis for judgements and allows decisions to be made.

Harvey (1998) illustrated this neatly: when the cook tastes the soup it is formative evaluation; when the dinner guest tastes the soup it is summative evaluation.

The terms 'feedback' and 'evaluation' are often used interchangeably, but the meanings are very different. Feedback is any information that is gathered and collated, by various methods and from different sources, and is only part of the attempt to establish the effectiveness of a course or programme of study. Evaluation, on the other hand, is the process by which all the feedback information is assembled and systematically scrutinised. It is only through weighing up the evidence that you are able to come to an overall judgement of effectiveness. This is important as it means that it is not just collecting feedback that is the evaluation, you actually have to analyse the information, form conclusions and then act on them for improvements in courses and teaching to be made. It is this latter half of the evaluation process that gets most overlooked and the analysis needs to be planned into the evaluation at the outset and in order to know what information needs to be collected.

It may also be clear from the similarities between evaluation and assessment that the attitude and response of staff to the various types of evaluation very much depends on what the evaluation is for and how it is done, with summative evaluation seeming punitive in many respects. In this chapter, we will very much focus on evaluation for the purposes of finding out about and improving one's own teaching and courses ('formative' evaluation), and this is also covered in more detail in Khan and Walsh (2006).

188

THE EVALUATION CYCLE

As we suggested in Chapter 2, evaluation and review is part of the course design cycle and should measure the effectiveness of all aspects of the design by drawing on a range of data types and sources. It should not be something that is tacked on as an afterthought. Evaluation and review is a process comprising four stages:

1   **Measurement** – systematic gathering of a range of data from a range of sources to measure the existing provision.
2   **Value judgement** – consideration of the significance and meaning of the various data, resulting in a judgement.
3   **Action** – implement changes if needed, based on the judgements and evidence, to further enhance the provision or to resolve any problems/issues.
4   **Monitoring** – check any changes to see if the impact is as planned.

This definition of evaluation and review – measure, judge, act and monitor – requires the consideration of a number of fundamental questions:

1   What are we trying to measure?
2   Which sources of evidence/data should we seek?
3   How can we obtain the information we need?
4   When should we carry out the measurements?
5   How will we act on the information?
6   Where will we report the results?

The following sections consider these six points separately.

1 WHAT ARE WE TRYING TO MEASURE?

To enable you to think this through it is useful to return to the course design cycle. In Chapter 2, we described it both as a diagram and as a series of questions. We will revisit the question version in Table 10.1, and add evaluation and review questions.

We are not suggesting that these are the only questions that you need to ask. We have provided some of the top-level questions, and you should be thinking about the teaching that you do and writing the specific questions that you need to ask. We are not suggesting that you need to

■ TABLE 10.1 Review linked to design

Design cycle

Design question	Review questions
Rationale	
Why are we doing this?	Should we still be doing this? In this way? For these students?
Aims and learning outcomes	
What should the learners be able to do?	Were these the appropriate targets, at the correct level and demand? Were they suited to the intake?
Content	
What content will be needed to achieve it?	Was this appropriate? Was it relevant and current?
Teaching/learning methods	
How are we planning to enable it?	Were they effective and efficient, with sufficient variety? Were there other options and opportunities?
Assessment	
How will we know that the learners have achieved the goals?	Were the methods used valid and reliable? What did the students achieve and at what level?
Environment	
What support will the learners need?	Was the support adequate? Is it sustainable? Can the students do more for themselves?
Management	
How will we make it happen?	Did it all go smoothly? Was the communication effective? What do the critical incidents tell us?
Evaluation and review	
How might it be improved?	Are these the best methods for measuring in order to assure and enhance quality?
Rationale	
Is this still valid?	Has the context – external and internal – changed? Is the course still fit for purpose?

look at all aspects at all times – we are in favour of a light-touch approach that is not bureaucratic as long as it does the job. However, we do need to think about which aspects we will review, and this should be based on the purpose of the review. There are several interconnected reasons for evaluating and reviewing any course or part of a course, to:

- check the 'health' of the course;
- improve a course for the lecturers as well as the students;
- explore a particular problem such as wastage, dropouts, poor results;
- monitor an innovation in a course such as the introduction of simulated laboratory work on a computer or the use of a VLE to promote preparation prior to seminars;
- aid reorganisation of a course – the content may be fine but the order is not;
- validate/revalidate a course, perhaps for an external body such as the Institute of Electrical Engineers, or the on-going review procedure dictated by the university;
- support applications for funding and staffing, particularly for a new course.

Many of these reasons will require that we look at a number of aspects of the course, but some may be more restrictive and, for example, lead us to focus on the assessment methods or the teaching and learning approaches only.

Lastly in this section, concerning what we are trying to measure, the checklist given in Table 10.2 may be of value to you. It is based on a list proposed by Miller (1987), but we have extended and related it to the model we are proposing.

2 WHICH SOURCES OF EVIDENCE/DATA SHOULD WE SEEK?

There are three main sources of evidence, as shown in Table 10.3. Feedback from these sources can be brought together with statistical data and information about the course, such as:

- course documentation;
- application/admission/attrition figures;
- examination results;

▓ TABLE 10.2 What to measure

Prerequisites

- What was I expecting – and what did they bring?
- What can I do about the gaps?

Aims

- What were the three/four most important things I expected my students to gain from this course?
- Is that what the aims say?

Learning outcomes

- Reflecting on what actually took place during the course, what attributes could my students have gained in terms of knowledge, skills and attitudes?
- Is this the same as I planned?

Content

- Was the content appropriate for the outcomes?
- Was any content redundant, not relevant or out-of-date?

Teaching and learning methods

- How and where did I expect my students to develop the attributes listed in the learning outcomes?
- Was the technology used appropriate?

Assessment and standards

- Did the assessment processes give each student an opportunity to practice and demonstrate what they could do (rather than illustrate what they could not)?
- Was the level and demand right, for the students and their qualification?

Links

- How did I illustrate the coherence within the course and the links to other courses in their curriculum?

Environment and support

- Did the students get the support that they needed, at the time that they needed it?
- Were the resources adequate?

References

- Did the students know which were the key references (annotated reading list) and were these materials available?

- details of courses in other institutions, for comparison;
- benchmark statements;
- access logs and tracking information on VLE or on-line learning package.

It is important to decide what can be gained from each of these, and then select the most fruitful for the review in hand.

TABLE 10.3 Sources of evidence

Source	
Who?	How?
Students	
– Current students	– Staff–student committees
– Former students	– Focus groups
– Students who have withdrawn	– Electronic or paper-based questionnaires
	– Interviews
	– Chat or discussion rooms
Peers	
– Colleagues and other teachers on the course	– Peer review/observation
– External examiner	– Exam boards and external examiners' report
– Professionals/professional bodies	– Validation and accreditations panels
Self	
– Self-evaluation based on own reflections on teaching	– Electronic or paper-based teaching journal, diary, log or 'blog'
	– Structured and systematic reflection using review checklists
	– Observation through videoing or taping own teaching

Triangulation

Many people have an interest in the quality and success of a course – e.g. the students, individual teachers, course team, department, institution, employers, professional bodies, funding councils, QAA. Each has a different stake and therefore will approach an evaluation from a particular perspective and will want different questions answered. This gives their views a certain bias, so in order to reduce the effect of this bias, it is necessary to collect information about the course from a diverse range of sources that reflect the vested interests of different stakeholders. To do this, it is necessary to have several viewpoints of the same 'event' and to triangulate their opinions.

Students may be the most appropriate source of information on some topics – clarity of the materials, access to resources – but they are not, however, in a position to comment about the currency and validity of the content. Nor can they gauge the standard/level of the material and this type of information is more usefully gained from peers, both within and beyond the institution. If you were to respond only to student opinion, you might lurch from one change to another, year on year, as requested by different cohorts of students, none of whom may then actually benefit from those changes.

3 HOW CAN WE OBTAIN THE INFORMATION WE NEED?

Feedback from students

Depending on whether you wish to obtain quantitative or qualitative information (or both) a range of methods is available to you – e.g. questionnaires, focus groups, interviews. In deciding which method(s) to adopt, you will need to consider how collection of the feedback is to be administered and this may depend on:

- The size of student cohort and the response rate that is acceptable – e.g.:
  - whether you want either to obtain feedback from the majority of students;
  - or to sample an opinion.
- How the information is to be analysed:
  - degree of automation required – e.g. use of software or optical mark reader;
  - nature of the comments desired as open-ended, written and verbal is much more enlightening but difficult and time-consuming to analyse.

- How the course is delivered so that you can administer the feedback method in a similar way – e.g.:
  - in a classroom for face-to-face teaching;
  - electronically for an online course.

Whether the feedback opportunities are organised as formal or informal events, you should explore how you can make use of some of the same technologies you use in your teaching to assist you in evaluation – e.g. an online questionnaire or chat room to gather responses. Online discussion rooms or chat rooms have the advantage of being able to create a 'transcript' of what is discussed. If you think you might struggle to capture everything that happens in a face-to-face focus group, it is worth thinking about making a video or audio recording of the event. A simpler and more interactive way of gathering feedback from your class is to use an electronic classroom voting system, if you have access to one, at the beginning or end of the teaching.

In any event, it is good practice to provide plenty of different opportunities for students to give you feedback about the course and to make these accessible in a range of formats. Don't forget that informal chats and out-of-class discussions with students can also provide useful, albeit anecdotal, feedback on your course and you should take this into consideration along with other more formal means when formulating conclusions.

Questionnaires

A number of question types can be used and some examples are given below. Each of these question types may be used to explore views, opinions, attitudes and suggestions for improving teaching.

Sentence completion

These questions tap a rich variety of responses and can be of the following type:

The main problem on this course is ....

What I enjoy most on this course is ....

The lectures on this course are ....

The main themes of this course seem to be ....

EXAMPLE: ELECTRONIC VOTING

In a module about music and theatre, the teacher used handheld voting devices (similar to a TV remote control which is pointed at a receiver) to gather feedback. Each student is given a handset and the results are recorded by the computer at the front of the room and converted instantly into a graph for display. This can be projected on to a screen for the audience and lecturer to view and respond to.

The session was used to review the module and to gather student feedback for the purpose of the module review.

Tutor reflections

After an initial discussion regarding module review, students were introduced to the system. They were talked through the handsets and receivers and were given the opportunity to get the inevitable excitement of using 'new toys' out of their systems. The first few questions were not related to module review ('Can you use the handset?', 'What is your favourite colour?', etc.) so that they could get used to submitting their votes before the important questions started. The results of each vote were kept hidden until all voting had been completed, at which time the results graphs were shown to the class and each was briefly analysed.

The responses were far more complete than paper-based answers often are, and there was none of the usual confusion over whether 1 or 5 meant excellent, as the words were shown on the screen where appropriate. It did not take long to set up or write the questions.

Ian Sapiro, School of Music, University of Leeds

Open questions

Open questions allow students to answer freely and therefore can elicit more considered responses. However, putting 'Any other comments?' at the end of a structured questionnaire tends to generate either no response at all or information that is unhelpful because it has no real relevance to the intended purpose. Open questions therefore need to be directed into specific areas that are of interest to the individual lecturer by using trigger questions. Analysing a large number of open questions is time-consuming, but the answers can be very revealing. The following are examples of open-ended questions:

- Which aspects of the course did you find most difficult?
- Are there any aspects of the course you feel you have not understood?
- Which two aspects of the course did you find most interesting?
- What two things did you like least about this course?

Rating scale

Rating scales allow students to give a grade, usually out of four or five options, in answer to a question. If the options are numbered, average scores for each question can be decided. Take care not to change the meaning of the scale around in a questionnaire as the respondents may not notice. Also, you need to consider whether the middle term in the rating range is 'undecided' or whether it has a particular meaning: we would suggest the latter. The following is an example of rating scale:

	POOR	FAIR	ABOUT AVERAGE	GOOD	VERY GOOD
The organisation of the course					
The demonstrators					
Compared with others, this lecturer was					
Explanation of difficult concepts					
Use of VLE					

Bipolar questions

Alternatively, bipolar (as the name implies) gives students the opportunity to rate whether an aspect is either at one end of the scale or the other, with you providing the descriptors. Examples of bipolar questions are:

Please place a tick at the appropriate point on the scale.

The tutorials were:

well organised	———————————	muddled
useful	———————————	waste of time
stimulating	———————————	boring

Binary questions

These allow for a simple yes/no or agree/disagree response:

Did you prepare well for the tutorials?	Yes	No
Did the laboratory work help to explain the theory classes?	Yes	No
The course was well organised	Agree	Disagree
The content was relevant	Agree	Disagree

Factual questions

It is not unreasonable to ask students for other information, assuming that you can accept and trust the responses:

- How many hours (on average) did you spend preparing for each lecture?
- Which books did you refer to?
- Which online resources did you refer to?

Monitoring using the VLE

You may wish to use information from your VLE to cross-check student responses. There are apocryphal stories of departments in which teachers put materials online for the students week by week so that they could

EXAMPLE: NATIONAL STUDENT SURVEY

The Higher Education Funding Council for England introduced a National Student Survey (NSS) in 2005 which was a questionnaire given to the majority of **final year** students between January and April. The stated aim of the NSS is 'to gather feedback on the quality of students' courses, to help inform the choices of future applicants to higher education, and to contribute to public accountability' (see www.hefce.ac.uk/learning/nss/). Examples of the types of questions asked are given below.

The teaching on my course	Definitely agree	Mostly agree	Neither agree nor disagree	Definitely disagree	Not applicable
1 Staff are good at explaining things					
2 Staff have made the subject interesting					
3 Staff are enthusiastic about what they are teaching					
4 The course is intellectually stimulating					

The full questionnaire is available at www.thestudentsurvey.com/ archive/questionnaire.pdf

revise regularly. At the end of the module, the students were asked whether having the materials online had helped them revise, and they returned a resounding 'yes'. The teachers were very pleased with this result until they checked the user tracking tools contained inside the VLE. From that, they drew reports of student usage of the materials week by week across the module. What they discovered was that students had barely looked at materials online in the first nine weeks of the module. In week ten, immediately in advance of the exam, the usage statistics shot up. Does this mean that the VLE supported a strategy of last-minute cramming?

Feedback from academic colleagues/peers

Peer observation of teaching

Peer observation of teaching is a valuable, and common, way of gaining feedback. And you may find that this is built into your probationary arrangements and/or teaching course that you are taking. You need to consider two obvious questions: 'who will observe?' and 'which class?' The answer to the first question is the more feedback the better, so ask anyone who is both willing to spend the time and who you think has good ideas and approaches to teaching and student learning. For the selection of session, it might seem easier to select a 'safe' class that you feel goes well. But this will probably tell you little about improving and enhancing your teaching, so set yourself a challenge.

Ideally, there should be several stages related to an observation – hence the need for someone who is willing to take the time:

- **Planning** – this meeting should set the ground rules: agree the class, the purpose of the observation, the records that will be kept, etc. A brief session plan should assist this meeting.
- **Observation** – for a class that lasts no more than an hour, all of it should be observed. If the class runs longer, you should have agreed in the planning meeting which part(s) would be viewed.
- **Reflection** – time for both the observer and the observed to think about the event. Meeting immediately afterwards means that all is fresh in everyone's mind, but it also means that you have not had time to think things through. The observed should jot down thoughts and impressions in preparation for the review meeting.
- **Review** – the time to talk about the class and share impressions and reflections. This should be led by the person who was observed, rather than be a post-mortem performed by the observer. Any records and notes made should be discussed, and an action plan related to any conclusions should be decided. It would be worth returning to the action plan, say, three months after in order to discuss progress.

It is useful if the observation is a two-way process – you observe each other. However, staying with the same observer for a period of time, while creating a 'comfort' zone, does not provide a challenge and fresh ideas.

Mentors

New staff are often assigned a mentor or adviser, and this person may deal with all aspects of your role: teaching, research and administration. A mentor can perform a number of useful roles, some of which are detailed in Table 10.4. Even if there is no formal mentoring scheme, it may be worth arranging a mentor, either within or outwith your department.

TABLE 10.4 The roles of mentors

1 Provide guidance and feedback on teaching sessions, approaches to other forms of teaching, assessment and student learning (expert: source of professional knowledge)

2 Explore and discuss self-assessments of preparation and teaching (mirror; supporter; coach)

3 Provide opportunities for observation of teaching (role model)

4 Help develop skills in teaching and related activities (coach and adviser)

5 Provide personal support where necessary and increase confidence (counsellor and friend)

6 Review progress (listener and, through questioning, challenger)

7 Act as a resource in terms of institutional and departmental policies, procedures and routines as they affect teaching and learning (resource person)

8 Help develop a reflective approach, whereby monitoring and evaluation, for improvement purposes, becomes an on-going process (guide and coach)

9 Assist development of a teaching portfolio (adviser)

Self-evaluation of teaching

Self-evaluation is an important part of developing your own teaching and is a key part of 'reflective practice'. Reflective practice (see Schön (1988 and 1991), Cowan (1998) and Moon (1990a, b and 2004)) is a mechanism by which you can systematically review your own teaching and continuously develop your practices. People naturally reflect on their experiences of teaching, particularly when they are new to it and less confident in their abilities, or when an experience has been painful. You will have come out of a teaching session saying to yourself that it went well or badly in an intuitive sense and this might be termed 'common-sense reflection'. In order to reflect formally on your teaching, you need to find a systematic way to articulate your reflections so that you can remember what you thought and build on that experience for next time. Possible ways that you can do this are by:

- keeping a diary, reflective log, learning journal, web log ('blog');
- analysing critical teaching 'incidents' (when things go wrong);
- making audio or video tapes of your teaching sessions and viewing/listening to them afterwards.

EXAMPLE: SELF-EVALUATION OF TEACHING

Module . . . . .   Lecture . . . . .   Date . . . . .

What seemed to work well?

What did not work as well as planned?

Next time I give this lecture:

I should omit . . .

I should change . . .

I should add . . .

Day, Grant and Hounsell (1988)

But how do you know whether it was good or bad – what was good or bad about it? You could review your own teaching practices against checklists or inventories of good practice or bring together your own reflections and the feedback from others (students and peers) with your reading of educational literature to formulate conclusions about your own practices.

4 WHEN SHOULD WE CARRY OUT THE MEASUREMENTS?

Courses can be evaluated at various stages, depending on what the evaluation is trying to achieve.

At the beginning (diagnostic)

Evaluating students' knowledge, skills and attitudes at the start of their course (really a form of assessment) may indicate:

- their approaches to learning;
- what their expectations and priorities are;
- their current state of knowledge;
- their understanding of the basic concepts;
- whether they have the necessary study skills.

This enables you to make adjustments about the content or delivery and tailor these to enhance the learning of a **particular** cohort by starting from where they are.

In the middle (formative)

Evaluation half-way through a course can be used to monitor:

- student understanding of the subject;
- appropriateness of the delivery;
- whether the learning outcomes are being met.

This enables you to determine whether changes need to be made while they can still be of benefit to the **current** cohort. It is an on-going responsive evaluation that demonstrates openness to students' problems and concerns.

TABLE 10.5 Feedback issues

Who will benefit?

If the evaluation is completed at the end of a block of teaching – the end of a module, perhaps – changes can only be made for the next cohort of students.

The respondents may not, therefore, be particularly motivated to contribute. This can be mitigated by undertaking a less detailed and quickly analysed mid-module evaluation that allows you to respond to immediate concerns and make any changes during teaching.

A colleague at Leeds transformed the students' approach to the end of module review by taking feedback half-way though his course and responding to the students' concerns, questions and impressions at that time.

How will students know the outcomes?

A major concern that students have about the evaluation process is that they fill in the forms and never discover the results. It is essential that we let students see that we take seriously the feedback that they give to us. Providing the details of changes/enhancements made to the course as a result of feedback from previous years is one way to do this. Including the information in handbooks, on course websites or telling them in the first, overview lecture of the course are all very good ways. This detail need not be restricted to changes/enhancements, there is no harm in explaining why changes have *not* been made, too.

Questionnaire fatigue

As noted before, students may be completing feedback forms on several parts of the course at the same time. 'Not another questionnaire!' Compound this feeling with a lack of knowledge about the results of giving this information (see point above) and we have the major problem of students not

At the end (summative)

Evaluation at the end of a course is used to ascertain how effective the student learning has been, to give an indication of the quality of the teaching and to assist in planning the course for the next time it is delivered. This type of evaluation does not benefit the current cohort but aims to improve the learning and teaching for the **next** student cohort. It should also bring together the outcomes from previous and other evaluations.

Timing of evaluation

If, initially, we focus on students as the source of data, there are a number of issues (Table 10.5) – some conflicting – that we must take

TABLE 10.5 (continued)

taking the process seriously. Knowing the outcomes helps, and it may be possible to reduce the scope/detail of the evaluation by taking a whole course/whole year approach to evaluation rather than the atomistic modular approach.

Evaluation before the assessment period

Some students are less likely to give useful and detailed feedback if they think – rightly or wrongly – that it could impact on the marking of their work.

This can be resolved by having the analysis done by a 'central' office rather than the individual member of staff, making the feedback a little more remote. Or by retaining the feedback sheets until after the assessment period before they are analysed. At the least, this should be discussed with students, rather than leaving them unsure.

'But the forms are anonymous,' you say. True, and that is an important part of the process, but many of us will admit to recognising at least some of the students either from the words they use, their writing or other ways.

Emphasise the anonymity, but still be willing to listen to the students' concerns over this.

Evaluation at module, year, programme level – which is best?

Hopefully, feedback will be taken at all of these stages in order to give several perspectives on a course. What must be avoided is the practice of adding up the results of the separate module evaluations and considering them as indicative of whole course review.

The questions at programme level should be very different compared to individual 'chunks'/modules of teaching. Also, students respond in very different ways when evaluating larger/smaller aspects of a course.

account of when making the decision as to the scope and timing of the procedure that we implement.

The other sources of data that were mentioned in the earlier section are less time-bound than taking comments from students, and should be collected at appropriate stages of the learning and teaching process.

If you only contribute to some aspects of a block of teaching, you may wish to discuss your contribution, and how it will be evaluated, with the leader of that aspect of the course. However, do not underestimate the value of informal methods of gathering data about the teaching/learning process: students are usually very willing, in informal settings, to give constructive feedback.

5 HOW WILL WE ACT ON THE INFORMATION?

We have suggested that evaluation and review involves measurement, value judgement, action and monitoring. Having collected a range of data from a number of appropriate sources, the information needs to be analysed and the messages it holds decided – both positive and developmental. We emphasise that this is a value judgement as you may be aware of factors that others are not, and you have to decide the priority and value that you give to the feedback. It may be that you need to gain more information in order to interpret the messages from a questionnaire. For example, what action do you take if:

1   85 per cent of the students tell you that the course was well-taught and that you explained the concepts well, but a colleague suggests that the work is not appropriate (too easy) for the level?
2   10 per cent of the students are negative about your teaching style?
3   55 per cent of the students say that the library provision was 'inadequate'?
4   50 per cent of the students consider the web pages that you provide to be 'unhelpful'?

As someone new to teaching in higher education, it will be worth discussing some of these issues with a more experienced colleague such as a teaching/probationary mentor.

You need to be aware that among others, Todd (2002) has reported that 'student evaluation can reveal more about gender biases than the quality of the tuition'. This means that both your gender and the gender mix of your classes can have an impact on the evaluation results – another good reason to triangulate data.

6 WHERE WILL WE REPORT THE RESULTS?

As we have already said, **acting** on findings from feedback is an integral part of the evaluation process. There is no point in conducting an evaluation if you are not going to do anything with the information you gather. It is also important to communicate the outcomes of any evaluation – not only the findings but the actions taken – back to those actually involved in the evaluation, and those with a stake in the outcome

– e.g. current and prospective students, programme teams, school management.

Examples of methods for doing this are:

- notices posted on student website or VLE;
- notice board;
- posters;
- in programme/module documentation.

This type of communication demonstrates the commitment of staff to the evaluation process and demonstrates to students that something is done with the information they supply. It shows them that their contribution to the evaluation process is valued and worthwhile. If students can see something positive being done in the light of their feedback, they will be more likely to make considered contributions to the evaluation process in the future.

EVALUATION FOR QUALITY ASSURANCE PURPOSES

As we noted above, one purpose of evaluation, particularly at the course level, is to fulfil the institution's internal quality assurance requirements. You will find that there is a procedure that all new courses – programmes and modules – have to go through before they are allowed to recruit students: an approval or validation process. The responsibility for the process will be at department and/or faculty level, and involve peer review, which for a new programme is likely to be an external referee. Similarly, there will be agreed processes for making changes to a course, and periodic checks – annual, periodic, quinquennial – through which modules and programmes are scrutinised in order to ensure that they provide a quality student learning experience. We recommend that you check what must happen in your institution, and so find out what part you have to play.

SUMMARY

In this chapter we have asked you to consider the why, when, how and who of evaluation and review, in order that you can monitor, assure and enhance the quality of your courses and your teaching. It is important that you familiarise yourself with the usual processes and practices of your institution, as there may be, for instance, a standard questionnaire that was designed and agreed by the staff–student committee. In addition, we have promoted the idea of using a range of indicators and feedback, including examination results, in order to inform the judgements that are made about the quality of the provision. Finally, we have suggested that you discuss the outcomes of the process with colleagues in order to benchmark the feedback that you get.

FURTHER READING

Evaluation Cookbook, edited by J. Harvey, is a practical guide to evaluation methods for lecturers. (LTDI) e-book: www.icbl.hw.ac.uk/ltdi/cookbook/contents.html

Kahn, P. and Walsh, L., 2006. *Developing Your Teaching: Ideas, Insight and Action.* London: RoutledgeFalmer

References

Allan, J., 1996. Learning Outcomes in Higher Education. *Studies in Higher Education*. Vol. 21, No. 1: pp. 93–108.

Anderson, L.W. and Krathwohl, D.R. (eds), 2001. *A Taxonomy for Learning, Teaching and Assessing*. New York: Addison Wesley Longman.

Atkins, M., 1995. What Should we be Assessing? In P. Knight (ed.), *Assessment for Learning in Higher Education*. London: Kogan Page.

Biggs, J., 1989, referenced in Gibbs, G., 1992. *Improving the Quality of Student Learning*. Bristol: TES.

Biggs, J., 1999. *Teaching for Quality Learning at University*. Buckingham: SRHE and Open University Press.

Biggs, J. and Moore, P. J., 1993. *The Process of Learning*. Sydney: Prentice Hall.

Bloom, B.S. (ed.), 1956. *Taxonomy of Educational Objectives: Handbook 1 – The Cognitive Domain*. New York: Longmans.

Bourner, T. and Flowers, S., 1998. Teaching and Learning Methods in Higher Education: A Glimpse of the Future. *Reflections on HE*, pp. 77–102.

Brennan, J. 2004. Making Progress on Progress Files. SEDA, *Educational Developments*, Vol. 5, No. 1.

Brown, G., 2001. *Assessment: A Guide for Lecturers*. No. 3, LTSN Generic Centre Assessment Series. York: LTSN.

Brown, G., 2004. How Students Learn. A supplement to the RoutledgeFalmer Key Guides for Effective Teaching in Higher Education Series. Available at www.routledgefalmer.com/series/kgethe/resource.pdf.

Brown, G. and Partington, J., 1995. *Effective Engineering Education*. Sheffield: UCoSDA.

Brown, G., Bull, J. and Pendlebury, M., 1997. *Assessing Student Learning in Higher Education*. London: Routledge.

Buzan, T., 2000. *The Mind Map Book*. London: BBC Publications.

Cameron, S., 2001. *Briefing Paper 2: Evaluating Internet Sites for Academic Use.* York: LTSN.

Carroll, J., 2002. *A Handbook for Deterring Plagiarism.* Oxford: OCSLD.

Chickering, A. W. and Gamson, Z. F., 1991. Applying the Seven Principles for Good Practice in Undergraduate Education. *New Directions for Teaching and Learning*, Vol. 47. San Francisco, CA: Jossey-Bass.

Chickering, A. and Ehrmann, S., 1996. Implementing the Seven Principles: Technology as Lever. *AAHE Bulletin*, October, pp. 3–6.

Cohen, L. and Manion, L., 1989. 3rd edn. *Research Methods in Education.* London: Routledge.

Cowan, J., 1998. *On Becoming an Innovative University Teacher – Reflection in Action.* Buckingham: SRHE and Open University Press.

Day, K., Grant, R. and Hounsell, D., 1998. *Reviewing Your Teaching.* Edinburgh and Sheffield: University of Edinburgh, TLA Centre/CVCP Universities' and Colleges' Staff Development Agency.

Dearing, R., 1997. Report of the National Committee of Enquiry into Higher Education. Chapter 9 – 9.14–9.54 Skills in Higher Education Programmes. Available at www.leeds.ac.uk/educol/niche/.

Dennis, N., 1990. Unpublished paper. Course design. Singapore.

DfES, 2005. The e-Strategy – Harnessing Technology: Transforming Learning and Children's Services. Available at www.dfes.gov.uk/publication/e-strategy/.

Downing, L. K. and Chim, T. M., 2004. 'Reflectors as online extraverts?'. *Educational Studies*, Vol. 30, No. 3, pp. 263–276. Available at http://journalsonline.tandf.co.uk/.

Doyle, C. and Robson, K., 2002. Accessible Curricula for All. Cardiff: University of Wales Institute. Available at www.techdis.ac.uk.

Duggleby, J. 2001. *How to be an Online Tutor.* Aldershot: Gower.

Earwaker, J., 1992. *Helping and Supporting Students: Rethinking the Issues.* Buckingham: Society for Research into Higher Education and Open University Press

Entwistle, N. 2005. Address to the British Journal of Educational Psychology Conference – Teaching and Learning in Higher Education: Contrasting Research Perspectives and Implications for Practice. University of Edinburgh, 19–20 May.

Exley, K. and Dennick, R., 2004. *Giving a Lecture: From Presenting to Teaching.* London: RoutledgeFalmer.

Gagné, R. M. and Briggs, L. M., 1979. *Principles of Instruction Design.* New York: Holt, Rinehart and Winston.

Gamson, Z. and Chickering, A., 1987. Seven Principles for Good Practice in Undergraduate Education. *AAHE Bulletin.* March, pp. 5–10.

Griffiths, R., 2004. Knowledge Production and the Research Teaching Nexus: The Case of the Built Environment Disciplines. *Studies in Higher Education*. Vol. 29, No. 6, pp. 709–726.

Harasim, L., 1989. Online Education: A New Domain. In R. Mason and A. Kaye (eds), *Mindweave: Communication, Computers and Distance Education*. Oxford: Pergamon, pp. 50–62.

Harden, R.M., 1986/1998. Approaches to Curriculum Planning. *Medical Education*. No. 20, pp. 458–466. Reprinted as an ASME Medical education booklet (21) and updated.

Harden, R.M., 1986/1999. Ten Questions to Ask when Planning a Course or Curriculum. *Medical Education*. No. 20, pp. 356–365. Reprinted as an ASME Medical education booklet (20) and updated.

Harvey, J. (ed.) 1998. Evaluation Cookbook. Learning Technology Dissemination Initiative e-book. Available at www.icbl.hw.ac.uk/ltdi/cookbook/contents.html.

HEFCE, 2001. Strategies for Widening Participation in Higher Education: A Guide to Good Practice. Available at www.hefce.ac.uk/pubs/hefce/2001/01_36.htm.

HEFCE, 2005a. Survey of Higher Education Students' Attitudes to Debt and Term-time Working and their Impact on Attainment. A report to Universities UK and HEFCE by the Centre for Higher Education Research and Information (CHERI) and London South Bank University. November. Available at www.hefce.ac.uk/Pubs/rdreports/2005/rd15_05/. Accessed 9 December 2005.

HEFCE, 2005b. Widening Participation in the UK. Available at www.hefce.ac.uk/widen/. Accessed 5 December 2005.

HEFCE, 2005c. Strategy for e-learning. Available at www.hefce.ac.uk/pubs/hefce/2005/05_12/. Accessed December 2005.

Jackson, M., 1997. But Learners Learn More. *Higher Education Research and Development*. No. 16, pp. 101–110.

Jary, D. and Jones, R., 2004. *Widening Participation: Overview and Commentary*. Higher Education Academy. Available at www.heacademy.ac.uk/resources.asp?process=full_record&section+generic&rid=513. Accessed 5 December 2005.

Kahn, P. and Walsh, L., 2006. *Developing Your Teaching: Ideas, Insight and Action*. Abingdon: Routledge.

Kaye, A., 1989. Computer-mediated Communication and Distance Education. In R. Mason and A. Kaye (eds), *Mindweave: Communication, Computers and Distance Education*. Oxford: Pergamon, pp. 3–21.

Knight, P., 2001. *A Briefing on Key Concepts*. No. 7, LTSN Generic Centre Assessment Series. York: LTSN.

Knight, P. and Yorke, M., 2003. Employability and Good Learning. *Teaching in Higher Education*. Vol. 8, No. 1, pp. 3–16.

Kolb, D.A., 1984. *Experiential Learning – Experience as a Source of Learning and Development*. Englewood Cliffs, NJ: Prentice Hall.

Kuethe, L., 1968. *The Teaching Learning Process*. Glenview, IL: Scott-Foresman.

Littlejohn, A. and Higgison, C., 2003. *E-learning Series – A Guide for Teachers*. York: LTSN.

MacDonald-Ross, G., 2004. *Plagiarism in Philosophy: Prevention is Better than Cure*. HEA Subject Network Philosophy and Religious Studies. Available at www.prs-ltsn.leeds.ac.uk/plagiarism/.

McSporran, M. and Young, S. (2001) Does gender matter in online learning?. *Alt-J*, Vol.9, No. 2, pp. 3–15.

Marton, F., Dall'Alba, G. and Beaty, E., 1993. Conceptions of Learning. *International Journal of Educational Research*, Vol. 19, No. 3, pp. 277–300.

Mason, R., 1991. Moderating Educational Computer Conferencing, *DEOSNEWS*, Vol. 1, No. 19. Available at www.ed.psu.edu/acsde/deos/deosnews/deosnews1_19.asp.

Mason O'Connor, K. and Oates, L., 1999. *Academic Tutoring*. SEDA Special No. 11. Birmingham: SEDA.

Miller, A., 1987. *Course Design for University Lecturers*. London: Kogan Page.

Monash, 2001. The list was based on ideas that were originally proposed by a group in the University of New South Wales (web pages no longer available) and this was added to by a discussion document circulated by Monash University. Available at www.celts.monash.edu.au/hedu/internationalising_the_curricu.html. Accessed May 2004.

Moon, J., 1999a. *Reflection in Learning and Professional Development – Theory and Practice*. London: Kogan Page.

Moon, J., 1999b. *Learning Journals: A Handbook for Academic, Students and Professional Development*. London: Kogan Page.

Moon, J., 2002. *The Module and Programme Development Handbook*. London: Kogan Page.

Moon J., 2004. *A Handbook of Reflective and Experiential Learning*. London: RoutledgeFalmer.

Newble, D. and Canon, R., 1989. *A Handbook for Teachers in Universities and Colleges*. London: Kogan Page.

NSW, 2002. The Faculty of Commerce and Economics at University of New South Wales, Sydney, used the structure to decide its approach to internationalising the curriculum. Available at www.fce.unsw.edu.ac/. Accessed 5 December 2005.

Oxford Centre, 1990: The Oxford Centre for Staff Development (now www.brookes.ac.uk/services/ocsd/). The table was included in open learning materials.

Paulsen, M., 1995. The Online Report on Pedagogical Techniques for Computer-Mediated Communication. Available at www.nettskolen.com/forskning/19/cmcped.html#v. Accessed November 2004.

Price, M. and Rust, C., 2004. Assessment Grid. York: Higher Education Academy Resources. Available at www.heacademy.ac.uk/resources.asp?process=full_record&section=generic&id=347.

Quality Assurance Agency, 1999a. Programme Specification. Available at www.qaa.ac.uk/academicinfrastructure/programSpec/default.asp. Accessed 23 November 2005.

Quality Assurance Agency, 1999b. Code of Practice for the Assurance of Academic Quality and Standards in Higher Education. Section 3: Students with Disabilities. Available at www.qaa.ac.uk/academicinfrastructure/codeOfPractice/default.asp.

Quality Assurance Agency, 2000a. Benchmark Statements. Available at www.qaa.ac.uk/academicinfrastructure/benchmark/default.asp. Accessed 23 November 2005.

Quality Assurance Agency, 2000b. Code of Practice for the Assurance of Academic Quality and Standards in Higher Education. Section 6: Assessment of Students. Available at www.qaa.ac.uk/academicinfra-structure/codeOfPractice/default.asp.

Quality Assurance Agency, 2001. The Framework for Higher Education Qualifications in England, Wales and Northern Ireland. Available at www.qaa.ac.uk/academicinfrastructure/FHEQ/EWNI/default.asp#annex1.

Race, P., 2005. *Making Learning Happen: A Guide for Post-compulsory Education.* London: Sage.

Ramsden, P., 2003. 2nd edn. *Learning to Teach in Higher Education.* London: RoutledgeFalmer.

Robinson, D., 2000. A presentation by Professor David, Vice-Chancellor of Monash University, *Monash 2020: Developing a Global and Self-Reliant University.* The talk was given at Toward the Global University II: Redefining Excellence in the Third Millennium, Cape Town, South Africa, 16–20 April.

Salmon, G., 1998. Developing Learning through Effective Online Moderation. *Active Learning*, No. 9. Available at www.ilt.ac.uk/downloads/031027_AL_Salmon.pdf. Accessed November 2005.

Salmon, G., 2000. *E-moderating: The Key to Teaching and Learning On-line.* London: Kogan Page.

Salmon, G., 2002. *E-tivities*. London: Kogan Page.

Schön, D., 1988. *Educating the Reflective Practitioner*. San Francisco, CA: Jossey-Bass.

Schön, D., 1991. *The Reflective Practitioner – How Professionals Think in Action*. London: Avebury.

Seale, J. and Rius-Riu, M., 2001. Introduction to Learning Technology within Tertiary Education in the UK. *Association for Learning Technology*, Oxford: Oxford Brookes University.

SENDA, 2001. A copy of the Special Educational Needs and Disability Act 2001 is available at www.opsi.gov.uk/acts/acts2001/20010010.htm. Accessed 4 January 2006.

Sheffield Project, 1993. A Conceptual Model of Transferable Personal Skills. Improving the Personal Skills of Graduates Project, 1989–91. Sheffield: University of Sheffield.

Todd, Z., 2002. Nice legs – Shame about the Teaching. *The Times Higher Educational Supplement*, No. 1, February.

Tresman, S. 2002. Towards a Strategy for Improved Student Retention in Programmes of Open, Distance Education: A Case Study from the Open University UK. *International Review of Research in Open and Distance Learning*, Vol. 3, No. 1. Available at www.irrodl.org/content/v3.1/tresman_rn.html.

UK Government, 2003. White Paper on The Future of Higher Education. Available at www.dfes.gov.uk/hegateway/strategy/hestrategy/.

Waterfield, W. and West, B., 2002. SENDA Compliance – An Audit and Guidance Tool for Accessible Practice within the Framework of Teaching and Learning. South West Academic Network for Disability Supports (SWANDS), University of Plymouth. Available at www.plymouth.ac.uk/assets/SWA/Sendadoc.pdf.

Weaver, M., 2006. Do Students Value Feedback? Student perceptions of Tutors' Written Responses. *Assessment and Evaluation in Higher Education*, Vol. 31, No. 3, pp. 379–394.

Wheeler, S. and Birtle, J., 1993. *A Handbook for Personal Tutors*. Buckingham: Society for Research into Higher Education and Open University Press.

Yorke, M., 1999. *Leaving Early: Undergraduate Non-completion in Higher Education*. London: Falmer.

Index

Pages containing relevant illustrations are indicated in *italic* type

Lightning Source UK Ltd.
Milton Keynes UK
UKOW06f0056120416

272054UK00011B/188/P

9 780415 380300